THE LAND OF THE SMOKIES

D1709994

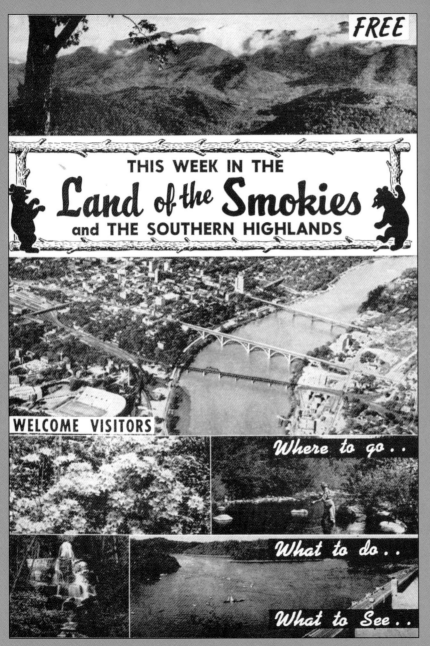

FREE

THIS WEEK IN THE

Land of the Smokies

and THE SOUTHERN HIGHLANDS

WELCOME VISITORS

Where to go . .

What to do . .

What to See . .

Guide booklets such as this one were published throughout the 1950s and 1960s; the coverage area they designated as the "Land of the Smokies" became the guideline for what is covered in this book.

The Land of the Smokies

Great Mountain Memories

TIM HOLLIS

University Press of Mississippi   Jackson

www.upress.state.ms.us

The University Press of Mississippi is a member of the Association of American University Presses.

Manufactured in China

Unless otherwise indicated, all illustrations are from the author's personal collection.

First Edition 2007

Library of Congress Cataloging-in-Publication Data

Hollis, Tim.

  The land of the Smokies : great mountain memories / Tim Hollis.
— 1st ed.

    p. cm.

  Includes bibliographical references and index.

  ISBN-13: 978-1-57806-943-9 (cloth : alk. paper)

  ISBN-10: 1-57806-943-2 (cloth : alk. paper)

  ISBN-13: 978-1-57806-944-6 (paper : alk. paper)

  ISBN-10: 1-57806-944-0 (paper : alk. paper) 1. Great Smoky Mountains National Park (N.C. and Tenn.)—History. 2. Great Smoky Mountains (N.C. and Tenn.)—History, Local. 3. Great Smoky Mountains (N.C. and Tenn.)—Description and travel. 4. Amusements—Great Smoky Mountains (N.C. and Tenn.)—History. 5. Tourism—Great Smoky Mountains (N.C. and Tenn.)—History. 6. Great Smoky Mountains (N.C. and Tenn.)—Biography. I. Title.

  F443.G7H57 2007

  976.8'89—dc22   2006025864

British Library Cataloging-in-Publication Data available

Contents

Introduction

About this time you are probably saying, "Oh, no! It's another of those crazy tourism histories from that Hollis character!" You're right, you lucky people you, and by now hopefully you are familiar enough with my other work that this one will need no explanation—or apology. Just be forewarned that if you have a low tolerance for rural dialect and cornpone humor, the pages that lie ahead make the *Beverly Hillbillies* sound like *Seinfeld*.

If it sometimes sounds like these corny pages are dripping with nostalgia rather than melted butter, it might be because the Great Smoky Mountains were my family's first vacation destination, way back in August 1966. My dad, my mom, my grandmother, and an aunt, plus the three-year-old budding author, piled into a 1964 Chevrolet early one morning and set out from Birmingham. According to the vintage road maps in my collection, Interstate 59 was more or less already complete at that time, which probably explains how we arrived in Chattanooga in time for breakfast.

Over the next few days we visited Gatlinburg—or at least I assume we did, since I have a single photo from that location; apparently we did not visit any attractions. Instead, we were en route to Cherokee, where we spent the balance of the time buying souvenirs and visiting the relatively new theme parks, Santa's Land and Frontier Land. In an example of how strange the human mind can

The author visited Rock City for the first time in 1967. Eleven years later, he returned to the same spot, older but no wiser.

FACING PAGE: By the mid-1960s, the base of Lookout Mountain had grown up to become a conglomeration of businesses all vying for tourists' attention. Some people considereed it roadside blight, but others (including the author) reveled in the sight.

The author (see if you can pick him out!) and family at a breakfast stop on Broad Street in Chattanooga, August 1966.

There is only one word to describe this photo of the author after his first visit to Cherokee, North Carolina: "UGH."

be—or even minds like mine—one vivid memory is of us stopping at a roadside souvenir store at which my parents bought a stuffed toy turtle for me. Why should I remember that forty years later? Beats me.

Somewhat oddly, in the years that followed, we did not visit the mountains quite as often as we went to the Florida beaches. We did "see Rock City" for the first time in 1967, but most of the rest of our mountain trips took place in the 1970s. Somehow, I always seemed to be aware of what was going on up in "them thar hills" anyway, probably because we continued to accumulate tourism literature even when we weren't actually there.

As a way of getting the preliminaries out of the way, let's go ahead and make the disclaimer here that what follows is not a scholarly approach to the subject of tourism in the Great Smoky Mountains. (Actually, you would have figured that out about two sentences into the book.) Many fine studies have already traced tourism's socioeconomic influence on this formerly isolated pocket of Appalachia and how area natives have frequently been at cross-purposes with those who would bring in more and more visitors from the great outside world. We will deal with a bit of that in our first chapter, but the main purpose for bringing it up at all is to hint at why doing the research for a book of this type was a bit difficult and frustrating at times.

In past books, I have written about how tourism history can be a challenging subject to document, largely because until about fifteen years ago, such a topic was not deemed worthy of preserving and because the southern brand of it was neglected for even longer than that. The same history in the Smokies is made even more complicated because so many of the locals have rather ambivalent feelings about tourism: they enjoy the prosperity that tourism has brought to them, yet they seem a bit suspicious of anyone who tries to dig too far beneath the outward appearance. As one astute resident put it to me, "We want your money, but we don't want you." Much of this attitude originates in the less-than-friendly way tourism was somewhat forced on the area, and some locals no doubt feel somewhat guilty about exploiting tourism for even not-so-ill-gotten gains.

Be that as it may, I forged onward even when it made me feel like a pigeon. (Ha, didn't expect that one, did you?) When the University Press of Mississippi and I first started making plans for this book, the intention was to have it center on the Great Smoky Mountains proper and that trio of tourism titans, Gatlinburg, Pigeon Forge, and Cherokee. We eventually decided to expand it beyond those perimeters and then had to decide just how to define our area. The answer came in the form of a series of tourism guides published during the 1950s and 1960s under the title, *This Week in the Land of the Smokies*. The magazine was based in Chattanooga and defined the "Land of the Smokies" as reaching from Boone and Blowing Rock, North Carolina, south to Lookout Mountain and its many sights. Not coincidentally, this turned out to be basically the same area encompassed by the association known as the Southern Highlands Attractions (except that the SHA includes a handful of tourist sites in southern Virginia). So, with those guidelines, this book resulted. If you notice an unusual amount of concentration on the aforementioned Gatlinburg/Pigeon Forge/Cherokee triumvirate, it is because so much of the business was concentrated in those three places. Notable sights and sites north and south of that area will be dealt with as we come to them.

Now, kick off your shoes and wiggle your toes to get comfortable, and let's set out for the former wilds of the Great Smoky Mountains. Don't be surprised if we encounter hillbillies, Indians, and bears along the way—and be even less surprised if they stop us for a few minutes to try to sell us a souvenir or rent us a room for the night. Things can get pretty ruthless from here on out, so keep one hand on the steering wheel and the other on your wallet, and let's go.

THE LAND OF THE SMOKIES

Thunder Keg

LARGEST 'STILL' EVER CAPTURED IN TENN.
This 1500 Gallon Still Was Found In The Loft Of
Large Dairy Barn In Knox County In May 1962
It Was Fired With Gas To Eliminate Smoke.
Captured With This STILL Was 432 Bags Of Sugar
10 Barrels Of Pure Corn Mash And 119 Gallons Of
120 Proof MOONSHINE Whiskey.
This Story Is True But The Names Are Not
Mentioned To Protect The GUILTY.

This photo shows why the Native Indians who inhabited this region gave it the name "big smoky mountains."

ONE

Thar's Gold in Them Thar Hills (And It's in the Touristers' Wallets)

At a crucial moment in the 1956 Broadway play (and later motion picture) *Li'l Abner*, the sleazy Senator Jack S. Phogbound pleads with the citizens of poverty-wracked Dogpatch, "You all is gonna be moved outa here by order o' the Newnited States government! Jes' remember—yo' government is spendin' one million dollars on one bomb, just to blow yo' homes off th' face of the earth! So show yo' 'preciation!"

Although intended as biting satire, the scene was not far from what had occurred in the real-life southern mountain country a couple of decades earlier. Unlike the beaches of Florida, which were largely uninhabited and uninhabitable until millionaires from the North turned them into winter playgrounds, the hills of Appalachia were teeming with families that had carved lives out of the rugged mountains. When tourism and all of its accoutrements drove in on the bumpers of cars, trailers, and campers, these indigenous individuals were not always welcoming.

Today, even when it is apparent that commercialism has become as much a part of the Smokies as the native black bears, many of those who make their livings off the tourist industry still have somewhat mixed feelings. In 2001, the A&E cable network devoted an episode of its *City Confidential* series to Gatlinburg, and during the show,

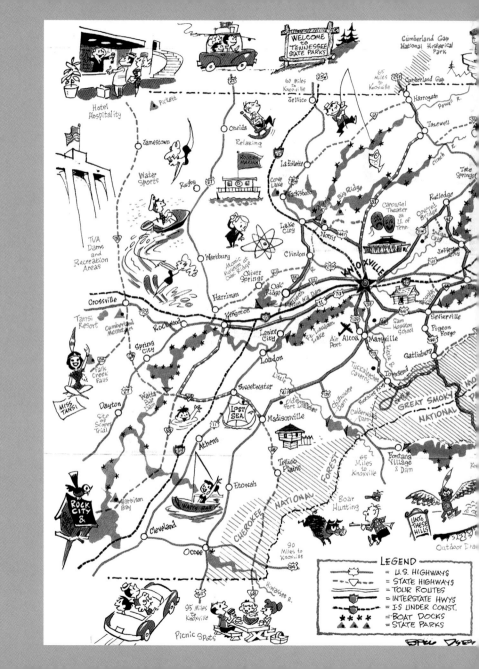

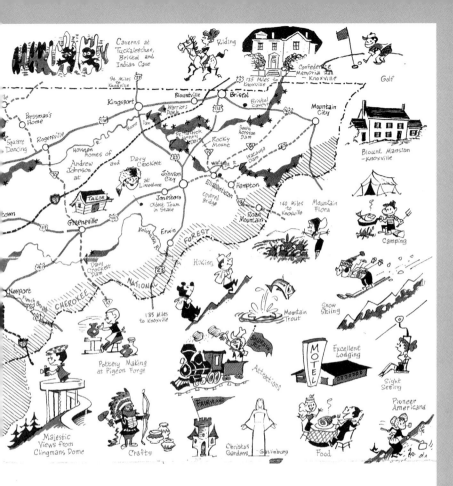

This highly entertaining map of eastern Tennessee gives a sneak peek at many of the sights we will see in this book.

one of the business owners remarked, "We'll put up with the traffic; we'll put up with you being in our way; we'll put up with you being rude to us sometimes; we'll put up with you not understanding what the area is like; because when you leave, we've got your money. And that's how we all look at it."

As we shall see many times in the following pages, this philosophy has been one of the primary driving forces in the attractions of the Smokies and their environs. Like practically any other industry, however, it started almost imperceptibly.

It would take an anthropologist to trace human habitation in the area that would later become the tourism capital of the southern mountains. Of course, the Cherokee Indians—who would themselves learn a thing or two about separating tourists from their wampum— had been in the region for centuries and would become the first to be forced from their homes to make way for so-called progress. In the grand old tradition of using life's lemons to make lemonade, this spot on the U.S. escutcheon would later become the basis for more than one profitable attraction in the area, as we shall see in later chapters.

The Cherokees' problems with the federal government notwithstanding, the story of the hill country's conflict between natives and tourists offers at least one glaring contrast to the story that unfolded along the Florida coastline. As documented elsewhere, that development came about because wealthy individuals from the North decided that balmy, subtropical Florida was a good place to escape the harsh winters. In the case of the southern mountains, although the wealthy invaded the existing homesteads, in this case the invaders were other southerners.

Anyone who has experienced the South in June, July, or August can attest to the fact that the magnificent outdoors can be a hot, humid, sticky, miserable mess. Now, just consider how things were in the 1800s, when there was no air-conditioning and the great

GATLINBURG
TENNESSEE

"ENTRANCE TO THE GREAT SMOKY MOUNTAINS
NATIONAL PARK"

MT. LE CONTE
ALT. 6,593 FT.

After beginning life as a crossroads hamlet named White Oak Flats, Gatlinburg, Tennessee, would come to be the centerpiece of the region's tourism industry.

The native black bears have been an integral part of the Smokies' tourism industry from the beginning.

WORLD FAMOUS BILTMORE HOUSE OPEN YEAR-ROUND EXCEPT NEW YEARS DAY, THANKSGIVING AND CHRISTMAS

The highlight of your mountain trip!

Biltmore House & *Gardens*

ENTRANCE ON US 25, ASHEVILLE, NORTH CAROLINA, VIA INTERSTATE 85, 26 OR 40

When George Vanderbilt chose to build his magnificent Biltmore estate near Asheville, North Carolina, he likely never envisioned that it would become a tourist attraction.

At one point, Asheville appeared destined to become the tourist capital of the southern hills, but by the time of this ad featuring North Carolina's Miss America 1962, it was obvious that the city was going to have to be content with the overflow from the other mountain resorts.

The Sight To See in Asheville

Unique among the great country houses of the world . . . chateau filled with fabulous Old World treasures: tapestries, paintings, porcelains, antiques, rare books. Thirty-five acres of formal gardens. Miles of landscaped drives. Beauty wherever you look.

BILTMORE HOUSE & GARDENS

U.S. 25—3 Mi. S. Of Asheville
Open 9 to 5 daily

DRIVE ON TO *Asheville*

LAND OF THE SKY

A Smoky Mountain visit isn't complete without vacation days spent in Asheville, scenic entrance to the Blue Ridge Parkway north. Tour famed Biltmore House . . . Thomas Wolfe's home . . . Biltmore Industries, world's largest hand weaving establishment . . . climb Mt. Mitchell, highest peak in the East. Excellent accomodations, with countless attractions and activities to make your stay memorable.
Retiring soon? Asheville's year-round mild climate and cosmopolitan atmosphere make it an ideal "home" for your enjoyment years.
For further information Write: L. S. Lindsey
Chamber of Commerce, Asheville, N.C.

Maria Beale Fletcher
Miss America, 1962
Invites You!

outdoors was about the same as the great indoors. This was an ideal environment for spawning all sorts of diseases, and people who were well off enough to look for a means of escape began casting their prosperous peepers on the comparatively cool and humidity-free mountain areas.

This trend began before the Civil War, when plantation owners from South Carolina and eastern North Carolina flocked to the mountains as a means of beating the heat. After the war, sanitariums sprang up to treat those afflicted with diseases such as tuberculosis, which was best handled in a less humid climate. For quite a few years, it appeared that Asheville, North Carolina, would become the hub of activity for this emerging culture. In 1888, multimillionaire George Vanderbilt chose Asheville as the locale for his sprawling country estate, which he named Biltmore.

Vanderbilt chose an appropriate name for his new domicile, because he certainly built more than most people had ever seen in their lives, let alone in a single residence. Although the property had enough opulence and amenities and covered enough acreage to be a small theme park, Biltmore remained strictly a private residence until 1931, when some of Asheville's business leaders convinced the Vanderbilt heirs to open sections of the estate to tourists. The timing of this move could be seen as a positive way to remind depression-era visitors of the prosperity that once was and could be again—or, in a more pessimistic vein, to remind them of what they could never hope to possess. Because people who were standing in bread lines typically did not take costly vacations, the former is probably the best guess.

Whatever the reasons, Biltmore continued to give visitors a taste of luxury for the next thirty years or thereabouts, but North Carolina historian Richard Starnes reports that the gild eventually wore off of even that lily: "By the 1950s the house and surrounding gardens

The Great Smoky Mountains National Park was created in pieces between 1926 and 1940.

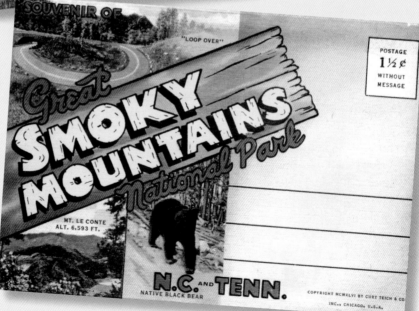

showed signs of wear and neglect," he said. "The Biltmore Company was losing nearly $250,000 per year. The costs of maintaining and preserving the house and its furnishings increased while the number of visitors declined." An all-out effort to get people to return to Biltmore began in 1960, and with the help of some of the Vanderbilt descendants, the house was renovated and promoted as the Asheville area's leading attraction. Starnes concludes that the estate did not again generate a profit until 1986, which probably helped the dearly departed George Vanderbilt to rest more easily in his grave.

While Asheville was apparently being primed for a leading role in mountain tourism, it would soon be demoted because of developments on the other side of the state line. As far back as 1899, there was talk of somehow getting the federal government to set aside land in the Appalachians—in particular, the Great Smoky Mountains—as a protected area. This had been done at Yellowstone and Yosemite way out west, but not until the creation of the national park system in 1916 did officials come up with an organized way of accomplishing these worthy goals.

The attempts to create a national park out of the Smokies had fitful starts and stops throughout the 1910s and 1920s. Part of the problem was that unlike most other federally preserved lands, which were pristine, unspoiled wildernesses, the Smokies had been settled long ago by hardy pioneer families. Although from a distance the mountains appeared untainted by human habitation, down in those valleys—those valleys so low—were farms and farmers. Getting multitudes of those folk, who were not known for being particularly fond of government in the first place, to agree to give up their lands was going to be a hard row to hoe.

The story obviously has two sides, and it is difficult to get an unbiased version of either of them. Press releases from the park modestly stated, "The Great Smoky Mountains National Park was a

$10 million gift from the people to the government. This was unlike the western parks, which were set aside by the government for the people." On the flip side were individuals such as Cades Cove resident Kermit Caughron, who at age seventy-two was interviewed on the occasion of the park's fiftieth anniversary in 1984: "I don't think it's something we should be celebrating, it took our home." There is, always has been, and likely will always be some disagreement as to whether the "$10 million gift" was given willingly or under duress.

One of the biggest boosters for creation of the national park was Knoxville wholesale druggist Colonel David Chapman, and his zeal rubbed some of the mountain residents' considerable fur the wrong way. Smokies historian Christopher Martin has related the story of how some of the Cades Cove inhabitants let their feelings be known by taking a wooden plank and burning a message into it: "Col. Chapman. You and Hoast Are Notify, Let the Cove Peopl Alone. Get Out. Get Gone. 40 M. Limit."

Ignoring this aspect of its history, a 1950 park publication itemized the twists and turns that took place—not just on the winding mountain roads—to bring the project about:

> The successful movement for the creation of a national park in the area was begun in 1923, and its establishment was authorized by the federal government by act of Congress approved May 22, 1926. Enabling acts were passed by the state legislatures of North Carolina and Tennessee in 1927, and land acquisition was begun with state funds, matched by a generous donation made by John D. Rockefeller Jr., through the Laura Spelman Rockefeller Memorial, in honor of his mother. Subsequently, federal funds were made available for the completion of the project.
>
> On February 6, 1930, the governors of North Carolina and

U.S. 441 loopily snakes its way across the national park from Tennessee to North Carolina, and postcards showing this view became quite common, probably because tourists would have found it difficult if not impossible to photograph this view themselves.

Tennessee presented the Secretary of the Interior with deeds to an initial 158,876 acres of land on behalf of their respective states. A limited park was thus established for administration and protection. The park, now containing approximately 505,000 acres of federally owned land, was formally dedicated on September 2, 1940, by President Franklin D. Roosevelt.

Those who are good at doing math will find a discrepancy between that last sentence and the fact that the park celebrated its fiftieth anniversary in 1984. This just indicates what a murky history truly does lurk in the smoky haze that gave the mountains their name. As for the purchase of private lands, the interview with Caughron pointed out that the event had additional overtones because the state was buying farms in the midst of the Great Depression, when many of the farmers were having trouble keeping body and soul together and had little choice but to sell. To add injury to

The highest point in the national park, Clingman's Dome, was named not for some pioneer's bald head but after Thomas L. Clingman, who first measured the summit in 1857.

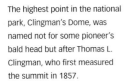

Maggie Valley, North Carolina, used an emblem whose sunbonnet-obscured profile made her appear to be the grown-up version of American Greetings's later famous Holly Hobbie character.

insult, the article further elaborated, "First National Bank in Maryville failed in January 1933, and many of the residents lost about half of the money they had deposited there from selling their farms."

All of this explanation serves mainly to help account for the odd relationship that exists in the Smokies between tourists and the people who live there. Little wonder that the main order of business is to get as much money out of as many people in as short a time period and with as little personal contact as possible.

The process had at least one bright spot. The big land grab largely excluded the members of the Eastern Band of the Cherokee Indians, whose reservation had been established on what would become the North Carolina edge of the proposed park between 1876 and 1880. The town of Cherokee had grown up as the capital of this subnation, and since the Cherokees had lost most of their land as a result of previous government hanky-panky, the reservation was, for the most part, outside the new development. Regardless, the Native Americans would undoubtedly reap benefits from its proximity to their lands.

Now, while all of this was taking place astride the Tennessee–North Carolina border, another national park was being established some four hundred miles north in Virginia. Officially established on December 26, 1935, Shenandoah National Park came to life at virtually the same time as its more southern counterpart. President Franklin D. Roosevelt's Works Progress Administration (WPA) put many otherwise unemployed people to work building a scenic highway to connect the two parks, creating a spinal column that would come

The Blue Ridge Parkway was established to connect Shenandoah National Park in Virginia with the Great Smoky Mountains National Park.

to link everything in between. The Blue Ridge Parkway transformed some isolated communities into what would become known in general terms as the Land of the Smokies.

Because people came to the region first and foremost to see the mountains, it should have been expected that some of the earliest attractions were based on natural rather than man-made features. Chimney Rock, for example, was one of nature's landmarks that gradually developed into a tourist center. The park's official history states that owner Jerome Freeman first built a stairwell to the top of the stone chimney in 1885. However, its modern tourism history began when Lucius Morse purchased the property in 1902.

Morse had come to the area as one of the innumerable tuberculosis patients who sought a cure in the Carolina hills. Recovered from that health setback, he set out to make Chimney Rock a destination, and he wasn't just blowing smoke. Even before the automobile era, Morse welcomed visitors who arrived by carriage or on horseback, and through the depression years, people continued to struggle up the 470 steps that led from the parking lot to the top of the magnificent chimney-shaped outcropping at the pinnacle.

Modernization came to Chimney Rock Park in the postwar years, and in 1949 the attraction debuted its much-welcomed elevator inside the mountain, which saved a lot of leg muscle strain. Since then, Chimney Rock has rocked on at a steady pace, adding features to benefit those interested in plant and animal conservation, and the park has remained at the forefront of tourism in its part of the state.

Not to be confused with Chimney Rock was Blowing Rock, which welcomed its first paying visitors in 1933. The brain behind the promotion of this otherwise obscure spot was Grover Robbins Sr. We shall be meeting his progeny—Grover Jr., Spencer, and Harry—in later chapters, as the three brethren carved out their own permanent places in southern tourism lore. As for Blowing Rock, it came equipped with lore of its own.

CHIMNEY ROCK

NO. CAROLINA

Chimney Rock Park, dating to 1933, was one of the first tourist attractions in western North Carolina.

Before World War II, those who wanted to venture to the top of Chimney Rock had to do so through sheer leg muscle strength. This elevator, added in 1949, put the wimpier tourists on a more even footing.

ELEVATOR

Entrance to the Tunnel Leading to Elevator, Chimney Rock, N. C.

K5698

BLOWING ROCK
U. S. HIGHWAYS 221 - 321
North Carolina

The Blowing Rock is an immense cliff 4090 feet altitude, overhanging Johns River Gorge with its valley 2000 to 3000 feet below. The phenomenon is so called because the rocky walls of the gorge form a flume through which the northwest wind sweeps with such force that it returns to the sender light objects cast over the void.

Blowing Rock took its name from the constant updraft coming from the valley floor far below. The park was a venture of Grover Robbins and his family, who would become intimately involved with mountain tourism during the 1960s and 1970s.

As one travels the highways of the United States, one legend is sure to pop up as often as Stuckey's billboards. This is, of course, the tale of the ill-fated lovers, which can be found in various forms everywhere from Silver Springs in Florida to Rock City on Lookout Mountain and beyond. Blowing Rock had its own version, which concerned itself with a Chickasaw chief's daughter who found herself living in the land of the Cherokees for one reason or another. Naturally, she fell in love with a handsome Cherokee warrior. Can you guess what happened next? Probably so, but here is how one of Blowing Rock's brochures told the legend:

> One Indian summer day they wandered toward the rock, where the Cherokee brave saw a strange reddening in the distant sky, which he took to be a warning of trouble. Duty came first and he declared he must return to the plains, but the maiden cried, "No, no!" In desperation he leaped from the edge of the rock down the abyss below. The maiden entreated him to come back, but he heeded her not. Then she prayed to the Great Spirit and to the wind, to blow her lover back. While she stood with outstretched arms, a gust of wind blew her lover back to her. Since that day there has been a perpetual breeze blowing from beneath the great rock—hence the name of Blowing Rock.

A later, and even more implausible, retelling of the legend has the princess praying for *days* before the wind finally returns her foolhardy sweetie to her embrace. Ignoring these tales, *Believe It or Not!* cartoonist Robert Ripley tagged Blowing Rock as "the place where snow falls upside down"—probably true enough because of the updraft from the valley far below.

It is one thing to try to determine the oldest attraction in the

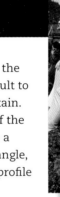

Grandfather Mountain

NORTH CAROLINA

U.S. 221 AT LINVILLE, N.C.—ONE MILE FROM BLUE RIDGE PARKWAY

Carolina's Top Scenic Attraction

U.S. 221

mountains by figuring out what year each one opened to the public, but for sheer age in and of itself, it would be difficult to argue with the craggy peak known as Grandfather Mountain. This name can be taken simply as an acknowledgment of the feature's age—estimated at one billion years, give or take a million or two—but in fact, when viewed from a certain angle, the ridgeline of the mountain does indeed resemble the profile of a bearded antiquarian looking into the sky.

Grandfather Mountain had been a member of the Morton family for decades by the time the modern tourism era arrived. Julian Morton's father established a resort at Linville in the 1880s, and Julian constructed a narrow road up the incline and a wooden lookout platform at one of the scenic stops in the early 1900s. After World War II, these original refinements were not holding up too well, and the rotting wooden stopover was more of a "look out!" platform. In 1950, Julian's son, Hugh Morton, took on the project of bringing his rocky grandfather into the mid–twentieth century: after making considerable improvements, he opened the modern-day version of the attraction in 1952.

A little imagination is required to see why the pioneers named this North Carolina peak Grandfather Mountain. Although visitors had been coming to Grandfather Mountain for decades, it did not become part of the modern tourism milieu until Hugh Morton purchased the property in 1952.

Grandfather Mountain was equally famous for its mile-high swinging bridge and its resident personality, Mildred the Bear. Hugh Morton says that Mildred was the only bear he ever knew who would allow a human being (in this case, Morton's daughter) to handle her cubs.

Morton has had a few chuckles over one bit of misinformation concerning the mountain. "When we first opened, we said the Indians had named it Grandfather Mountain because of the face on the ridge," he said. "Then, some experts pointed out to us that such could not have been the case, since the Indians did not have beards. We now say the pioneers named the mountain. Sometimes you to have to change things to be more accurate."

Over the years, Morton used his ever-increasing influence with state authorities to improve Grandfather Mountain's standing and likewise benefit the general public. When the Blue Ridge Parkway was nearing completion in 1968, the only segment left to be constructed was the proposed route over Grandfather. Morton was determined that not a single boulder or tree on his peak be disturbed, and the government was forced to explore other avenues. Compromise was finally reached in 1987 by building the Linn Cove Viaduct around the mountain's surface, preserving the natural beauty and receiving national recognition for its ingenuity. Morton constantly remained on his guard. During the 1970s, a nearby mountaintop suddenly sprouted a monstrous condominium on its peak, which stuck out like a sore thumb in the magnificent view from Grandfather Mountain's summit. Morton pushed hard, and in 1983 his efforts helped lead to the passage of what became known as the "Ridge Law," which required that any building constructed on a mountain could not extend more than three stories above the ridgeline. Morton's determination to preserve the sanctity of the surrounding landscape might have irritated some would-be developers but certainly did its part to help insure that visitors to Grandfather would always have something worth looking at.

For years, the most famous sight at Grandfather Mountain, aside from the view, was Mildred the bear. Mildred arrived at the park in 1968 after spending the first two years of her life at a zoo in Atlanta. Morton originally intended to release Mildred into the wild to do her part to replenish the Smokies' declining black bear population. However, because Mildred had never lived in the wild, she preferred wandering the park grounds and watching the tourists who were watching her.

Morton came to love Mildred as much as one of his own children; renowned photographer that he was, he made a second career out of documenting her life in pictures. When Mildred was found dead of old age in her den on the first morning of 1993, a little of Morton and the rest of the southern tourist industry died with her.

With the formidable trio of Chimney Rock, Blowing Rock, and Grandfather Mountain, North Carolina might have seemed to oc-cupy a position from which it could crow over neighboring Tennessee when it came to natural attractions. It is true that the mountains on Tennessee's side did not produce the same type of formations, but that state made up for it in another way. Instead of sending its tour-ists into the clouds, Tennessee buried them underground.

Caves have been and always will be one of the most durable forms of roadside attraction. The challenge for the owners of each cavern was to find some way to make theirs somehow stand out from the rest of the crowd. One near Sweetwater, Tennessee, had a distinct advantage. Its marketing director, Andy Smalls, commented, "There was a gentleman named William Sands who used to play in that cave when he was a little boy, back around 1911 or 1912. It was just a little hole in the wall on the Sweetwater side. He and his bud-dies would go in and out, and one day after a big rain he heard this water back behind there. Somehow he got up the courage to go down under a ledge and found this six and a half acre lake inside the cave.

SAIL THE LOST SEA TENNESSEE

All his life he told people there was water back there, but he didn't know how much."

After about fifty years of trying to convince people of the lake's existence, Sands finally sold the property to an attorney from Knoxville who enlisted the help of advertising man Charlie Tombras in opening the attraction to the public. In June 1965, the Lost Sea found its first paying customers. Lights were installed under the water to help illuminate the vast "sea." At a certain point during the tour, conducted by flat-bottom boat, the lights would be extinguished to prove Smalls's contention that "there's no darker dark than the inside of a cave. After we'd turn the lights off, pretty soon we'd hear people screaming and have to turn them back on again!"

Sail Tennessee's
LOST SEA
...in famous glass bottom boats

WORLD'S LARGEST UNDERGROUND LAKE

Sail the
LOST SEA

WORLD'S LARGEST UNDERGROUND LAKE!

- Glass bottom boat rides
- Deep inside Craighead Caverns
- Crystal clear, natural wonder
- Home of the prehistoric jaguar
- Other cave mysteries

CONTINUOUS TOURS DAILY—STARTING 8 A.M.

5½ MILES EAST OF SWEETWATER OFF U.S. 11 AND WEST OF MADISONVILLE OFF U.S. 411

Charlie Tombras and his group of investors opened the Lost Sea, near Sweetwater, Tennessee, in 1965. The ads and billboards for the Lost Sea used this Viking ship logo (left), confusing many tourists who came to expect a ride in something more exotic than a flat-bottomed dinghy.

Crystal Cave advertised that it was "Chattanooga's Best Attraction or Your Money Back." Judging from the condition of this sign, it must have had to return too many people's money.

The Lost Sea joined Rock City Gardens as one of the most aggressive advertisers on U.S. Highway 11. "Charlie Tombras was a genius at advertising," says Smalls. "He got the idea that there were so many things to tell about the Lost Sea that you couldn't fit it all onto one billboard. And it was the people coming from Florida and going back to Canada that we wanted. Charlie poured 100 percent of the money into billboards, and he patterned them after the old Burma Shave signs. On one billboard he would put LOST SEA, PREHISTORIC ANIMALS; on the next one, RESTAURANT; the next one, GIFT SHOP; the next one, GIANT BLIND RAINBOW TROUT—well, they weren't blind, because I was there when they caught the fish and put them in there!—but by the time you got there, you had to stop and see this thing!"

For reasons unknown, the Lost Sea billboards chose to promote the main feature with artwork of a Viking ship, leading tourists to expect something somewhat more exotic than the true boats featured at the site. Nevertheless, the U.S. Department of the Interior designated the Lost Sea as a registered natural landmark in 1976, and it continues to find—rather than lose—tourists to this day.

Around Chattanooga, at least four different caves were developed for commercial purposes. Mystic Caverns, opened in 1960, simply claimed to be "America's most mysterious underground caverns," with no authoritative data to back up that statement. Crystal Caverns was a bit more novel, using a gondola to transport its visitors twenty-eight hundred feet to the top of Mount Aetna, where they toured a replica Indian village before sending them into the caverns' depths.

Wonder Cave had reportedly been around as an attraction since 1900 or so but also claimed to be the oldest caverns in the South. "Used for centuries by the Cherokee Indians, the crystal clear 'River of Mystery' flows out, forming the 'Big Spring,' where eyeless fish and crawfish are found," Wonder Cave promotional literature marveled in 1963. Some years later, Raccoon Mountain Caverns stole stealthily into the tourism market like the ring-tailed rodent from which it took its name, taking over Crystal Caverns's former turf.

In the immediate neighborhood of the Great Smokies, two more formations battled it out under the surface. Tuckaleechee Caverns at Townsend came up with the not-to-be-challenged slogan of "Greatest Sight under the Smokies." The development of Tuckaleechee (an Indian word meaning "peaceful valley") is credited to Bill Vananda and Harry Myers, who opened the caverns to the ever-increasing crowds around Gatlinburg in 1953.

Tuckaleechee's nearest competitor was Forbidden Caverns, east of Sevierville, which crawled out of its hole in the ground in 1967. This attraction took its ominous name from what it termed an "ancient Cherokee legend" concerning one of those many lost Indian princesses of fable, somewhere in which was found the warning, "To the north of Snake Back Mountain, to the east of Rocky River, lies a place that is forbidden, hollow mountain of two streams." That was good enough for the tourist biz, and Forbidden Caverns was soon playing up its macabre Grotto of the Dead and Grotto of the Evil Spirits with special lighting and stereophonic sound effects.

Wonder Cave, on U.S. 41 north of Chattanooga, wowed tourists beginning at the turn of the twentieth century. The opening of Interstate 24 eventually did in the attraction.

SEE BEAUTIFUL
WONDER CAVE
OF TENNESSEE.

— Open All Year —
• ANTIQUE & SOUVENIR SHOPS •
• FREE PICNIC AREA •

Outstanding for the tremendous amount of live onyx formations & great diversity of interest, Wonder Cave is the South's oldest & most beautiful caverns. Its beautiful structures are enjoyed since they are concentrated within an easily traveled area. Used for centuries by the Cherokee Indians, the crystal clear "River of Mystery" flows out, forming the "Big Spring", where eyeless fish and crawfish are found. The temperature is always 56°. Beautiful new entrance building with spacious lounge.

• Stay on U.S. 41 to see Wonder Cave. Do not take Interstate 24 •
—On U.S. 41, 52 Mi. North of Chattanooga & 84 Mi. South of Nashville—4 Mi. North of Monteagle, Tenn.

"PRIEST AT ALTAR"

Forbidden Caverns sent out these photos of an unidentified movie being filmed in its chambers. We don't know what the story was, but it looks like Fred Flintstone got up on the wrong side of the cave.

Because of their proximity, Linville Caverns, Grandfather Mountain, and Blowing Rock occasionally produced joint advertising materials.

Linville Caverns
OPEN ALL YEAR
US 221 4 MILES SOUTH OF THE BLUE RIDGE PARKWAY
18 MILES NORTH OF MARION, NORTH CAROLINA

FEATURING THE MILE HIGH SWINGING BRIDGE
GRANDFATHER MOUNTAIN
LINVILLE, NORTH CAROLINA

Blowing Rock
US Highways 221 - 321
NORTH CAROLINA

For its part, North Carolina expended little effort to compete in the great cave sweepstakes, although Linville Caverns was near enough to both Grandfather Mountain and Blowing Rock to lure some of the visitors to both spots. In the 1950s, Linville Caverns not only shared tourists with its neighbors but also participated in three-way joint brochures with them.

Until the late 1960s, most people who visited the southern mountains came by way of one of the major federal highways. U.S. 11 was a real lifeline for the area, coming up from Birmingham, Alabama, through Chattanooga and Knoxville and onward into Virginia. U.S. 41 brought visitors from the Midwest into Chattanooga but then became principally a route to Florida. Of course, we cannot forget U.S. 441, nicknamed the Uncle Remus Route, which was the main drag passing through Sevierville, Pigeon Forge, Gatlinburg, and (after cutting through the national park) Cherokee and other points south.

Much of this changed with the implementation of President Dwight D. Eisenhower's interstate highway program in the late 1950s. Of course, it took a while for the system to make noticeable progress, but in 1967, a visitors' guide elaborated, "The new interstate highways will make it possible for many summer visitors to the Smokies to make the trip in less than a day, giving them an extra day or two in the area. Interstate Highway 75 is the leading highway funneling visitors to the Smokies. It extends from the northern tip of Michigan to Tampa, Florida, a distance of 1,627 miles. It is 85% complete and brings visitors from the north-central states, Georgia, and Florida."

Because the most mountainous areas remained off the interstates' beaten paths, this new form of transportation had fewer adverse effects on local attractions than was the case in Florida, where scores of businesses closed because the traffic had been siphoned away from them. People still had to leave the interstates to get into Gatlinburg and other such resorts, so the highways had mostly beneficial effects—as the press release indicated—by making it easier for people to get there. One of the few casualties was Wonder Cave, which depended heavily on the tourist traffic of U.S. 41. Being bypassed by I-75 was just too much for Wonder Cave—no wonder!

By the time the interstate highways came to town, the Great Smoky Mountains National Park had developed its ongoing reputation as the most heavily visited installment in the entire national park system. Even so, it sometimes seemed to have problems getting any respect outside of its own area. For example, in 1958, the Disneyland Records label released an album titled *Songs of the National Parks*. Narrated by veteran actor and singer Thurl Ravenscroft, the LP took listeners on a tour of the nation's parks but never mentioned the Great Smoky Mountains. (Other southern parks, including Shenandoah and the Everglades, received single, brief references.) Instead, the album focused on the parks of the West, as if all the trouble to put the land together for the Great Smokies park had never taken place.

(To be fair, it should also be mentioned that Disney's music division enjoyed some success with a song called "Farewell to the Mountains," with lyrics supposedly written by Tennessee's famed native son, Davy Crockett, as he prepared to leave his home turf. At any rate, the Disney productions about Crockett, some scenes for which were filmed on location in western North Carolina, brought more attention to that part of the country than a single record album would have.)

No matter how people got there, all of the tourist hot spots attracted crowds, but once folks were in the area, it was advisable to have other things for them to do as well as places for them to sleep, eat, and get gas (hopefully the last two were not in the same business). As we move along, we will next take a look at how some crafty handicrafters were among the first to find ways to spin straw into gold—or at least, nickels and dimes.

In the unusual artwork for this brochure, friendly bunnies and other forest folk join tourists in watching bears with Mickey Mouse ears.

U.S. 441 was the lifeline not only of Pigeon Forge, Gatlinburg, and Cherokee but also, as this map shows, of much of the rest of the South's tourism industry.

THE SCENIC ROUTE
BETWEEN THE
MIDWEST AND FLORIDA

U.S. 441

UNCLE
REMUS
ROUTE

THROUGH THE GREAT SMOKIES

MILEAGE FROM THE
GREAT SMOKIES

From Gatlinburg:

Cherokee, North Carolina	32
Tallulah Falls, Georgia	107
Milledgeville, Georgia	246
Dublin, Georgia	294
Douglas, Georgia	370
Lake City, Florida	473
Ocala (Silver Springs), Florida	558
Orlando, Florida	637
St. Petersburg, Florida	661
Lake Wales, Florida	675
Palm Beach, Florida	812
Fort Lauderdale, Florida	853
Miami, Florida	871

POINTS OF INTEREST
ON U. S. 441

Norris Dam (TVA) and Lake

Oak Ridge—The Atomic City
(16 miles from Knoxville)

Pigeon Forge, Tennessee:
    Fort Weare—Animal Park
    Pigeon Forge Pottery

Gatlinburg, Tennessee:
    Outdoor Drama—"Chucky Jack"
    Ride The New Sky-Lift
    Homespun Valley Museum

Great Smoky Mountains National Park

Cherokee, N. C.:
    Drama "Unto These Hills"
    Cherokee Indian Reservation
    Ancient Indian Village

Thru Georgia:
    Tallulah Gorge and Lake
    Black Rock State Park
    Antebellum Homes
    Lake Sinclair—Georgia's largest
    Eagle Rock Park—4-H center
    Okefenokee Wildlife Park
    Famous Suwannee River

Thru Florida:
    Stephen Foster Memorial Park
    Unique Silver Springs
    Lake and Citrus section
    Lake Okeechobee
    Palm Beach and Miami

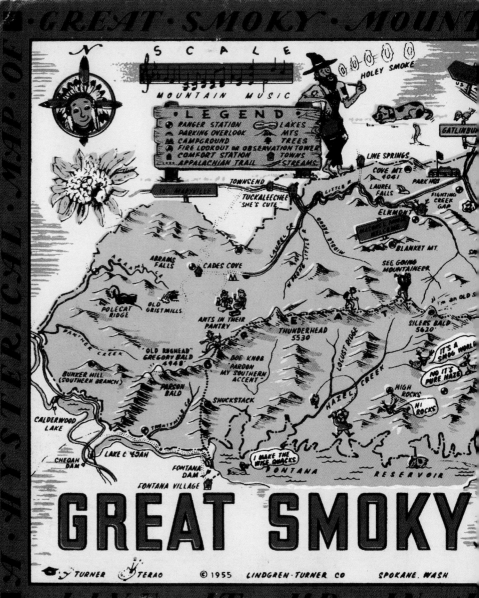

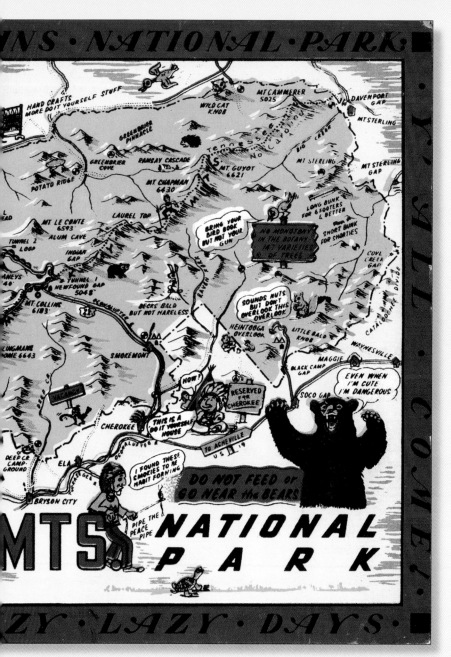

This gag-filled map of the Smokies was issued as both a postcard and a full-size wall poster. (Warren Reed Collection)

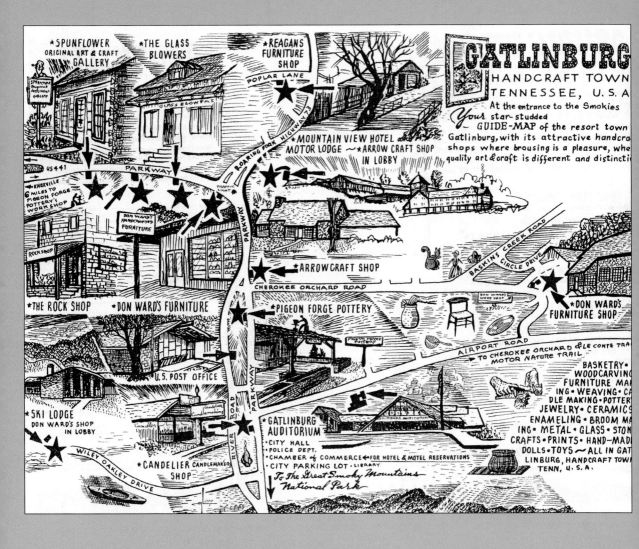

Crafts an' Vittles an' Sich

Long before the Great Smoky Mountains National Park was officially established, there had been some activity in the vicinity of what was then a tiny mountain community called Gatlinburg. Whereas Asheville was developing as the seat of culture and refinement on the North Carolina side of the mountains, on the Tennessee side Knoxville tried to be the leader in all things wealthy. Some of that city's more well-to-do residents discovered that a trip into Gatlinburg—en route passing through the equally microscopic burgs of Sevierville and Pigeon Forge—was charmingly exotic.

Although it seems to be a matter of academic opinion as to whether the inhabitants of the mountains were actually as backwoodsy as was reported (since that was largely a matter of perception), in 1912 the Pi Beta Phi sorority chose Gatlinburg as the site of a school. The high-minded ideal was to teach the mountain folk the ways of the modern world—whether or not they wanted any part of it. In 1981, the Gatlinburg newspaper gave an account of what happened next and how it would come to have far-reaching effects on the area: "The school staff, headed by Miss Evelyn Bishop, was interested in native crafts and their possibilities for the mountain people. They saw, in many homes, the beautiful things made by the grandparents, and were quick to realize the value of old coverlets and other treasures. In 1915 an arts and crafts program was started at the

FACING PAGE: Before the weird museums, before the miniature golf courses, before the motels, Gatlinburg was known for its local handicrafts.

TOP: Much like shopping malls in more urban areas, sprawling complexes such as this one housed Gatlinburg's craft industry.

CENTER: Aunt Mahalia's is generally recognized as the oldest candy concern in Gatlinburg. The ad at left dates from 1948; the photo shows one of the red-and-white striped outlets as they appear today.

BOTTOM: The Ole Smoky Candy Kitchen was another long-standing Gatlinburg goody maker. As in the neon sign and paper bag design here, cute bears were a major part of its logo. (Rod Bennett Collection)

school to encourage the production and improvement of handmade things, especially weaving and baskets."

We hope you weren't looking out the window at the dogwoods and daydreaming just then, because you might have missed the key word in all of that: *improvement*. The Pi Beta Phi do-gooders did indeed come up with the idea of having their charges manufacture handicrafts for the retail trade but did not consider it absolutely necessary that those crafts be the same as the ones that had been produced for generations. No sirree, Bob, the traditional methods were combined with new ideas to make the seemingly rustic objects more artistically pleasing, and the craft industry of the Great Smokies was birthed.

Pi Beta Phi opened a shop to sell its students' new old-fashioned creations. That store, named the Arrowcraft Shop, has survived to this day. Crafts soon became the primary industry not only in Gatlinburg but also in the rest of Sevier County. By the time the post–World War II tourism boom hit, the area was ready. In 1946, Douglas and Ruth Ferguson opened the Pigeon Forge Pottery enterprise in Pigeon Forge, which up to that time had not even been a very wide spot in the road. Two years later, the Southern Highland Handicraft Guild chose Gatlinburg as the site of its first Craftsman's Fair. The idea of crafts expanded beyond the traditional implements of farm and home—mainly quilts, baskets, and pottery—to include offshoots such as candles, woodcarvings, furniture, and candy.

Oh yes, the candy. That would come to be another big part of Gatlinburg's industry over the years, and supposedly it all began in 1939 with Aunt Mahalia's. (If there were candy stores in the area prior to that, their names remain mired in the past as if it were molasses.) Aunt Mahalia's operated for decades on a prime corner of Gatlinburg real estate, out of a building that was impossible to ignore. Its loud red and white striped canopy was reminiscent of a candy cane, and the roofline featured lighted figures representing the store's various wares. Aunt Mahalia's is still around, although it has taken on the form of a series of smaller storefront locations. Tradition is maintained by the facades continuing to sport red and white stripes and smaller unlighted versions of the figures that once crowned the original location.

Aunt Mahalia was merely the vanguard for the great candy invasion. It almost seemed that lacking a sweet tooth should have been a criminal offense in the Gatlinburg legal code, so prevalent did these tempting treats become. The Ole Smoky Candy Kitchen's logo was a trio of bears cooking up treats; the company now sells its "taffy logs" (a more mountainous name than saltwater taffy) across the country. Would-be candy tycoons didn't budge when it came to fudge, either, with the gooey goody on sale in practically every conceivable location. In 1959, those who preferred natural sweetness could visit Gatlinburg's Honey Bee Shop, which deftly blended its product with hillbilly humor: "Come on in git yore honey whilst you'ns watch— The bees make hit cause we'uns ain't aimin to sting you."

The explosion of crafts and candy was felt all the way across the mountains in the Native American bailiwick of Cherokee. Some of the tribal leaders must have been paying attention to what was going on over there in Tennessee, because in the 1930s, the town began to grow its own peculiar brand of craft shops. Whereas the mountain folk around Gatlinburg and Pigeon Forge manufactured items that could reasonably pass for pioneer relics, in Cherokee the populace concentrated on those items that most loudly screamed "Indians" to those whose main exposure to such culture was at the local movie house.

In fact, the Cherokee crafts industry appears to have been modeled somewhat after that of Western tribes such as the Navajos, whose hawking of wares to passing tourists had become a part of

On the Tennessee side of the mountains, baskets and quilts were big in the crafts field; in North Carolina, shops such as these marketed moccasins, feathered headdresses, toy drums and tomahawks, and other Indian accoutrements.

When tourists began flocking to the new national park, the denizens of Cherokee, North Carolina, began to see that they could make plenty of wampum.

The Cherokee Chieftain Craft Shop, Cherokee, N. C.

VISIT THE **TOMAHAWK SHOPS** IN CHEROKEE
Finest selection of Indian and Mountain Crafts — Indian Baskets,
Pottery, Beadwork, Moccasins, Tomahawks, Blow-Guns
and Gifts and Souvenirs of the Smokies

Homer and John

SOUVENIR FOLDER
of **CHEROKEE**
INDIAN RESERVATION
NORTH CAROLINA

CHIEF AND MEDICINE MAN

FOOTBRIDGE ACROSS OCONALUFTEE RIVER

COPYRIGHT MCMXLVI BY CURT TEICH & CO., INC., CHICAGO, U.S.A.

PLACE
STAMP
HERE

All items manufactured on the Cherokee reservation were supposed to bear this tag of authenticity.

American folklore. (Remember the old gag? "While I was in New Mexico, I bought an old Indian blanket. Of course, it was pretty crowded in there with the old Indian.") The Cherokees manufactured moccasins, toy tomahawks and drums, feathered headdresses, and anything else that looked remotely appropriate. To ensure authenticity, all genuine items were supposed to carry a tag confirming that they had indeed been made on the official reservation.

As the crowds visiting Cherokee increased, another form of business venture emerged that was—and still is—difficult to classify. It did not strictly fall under the heading of crafts, but it also did not operate in the same fashion as a motel or tourist attraction. The name of this business was "chiefing," and its evolution says a lot about what the public came to expect.

Somewhere along about the time World War II ended, Cherokee resident Carl Standingdeer decided that he was missing out on a great opportunity. Securing an elaborate headdress—the type worn by the Plains Indians, not the Cherokees—he offered to pose for photographs with tourists in exchange for tips: in other words, he was getting paid to have his picture taken. "Chief" Standingdeer soon found that this was a most lucrative job, and postcards and tourist literature dubbed him the "world's most photographed Indian."

In the 1950s, more and more Cherokees decided that they wanted a career in chiefing. Their outfits ranged from the simple—some photos of Standingdeer show him wearing the headdress with a standard white shirt and tie and black trousers—to the elaborate, especially in their head wear. For some years, the headdresses were fashioned out of eagle feathers, but in 1954, when it became illegal to ill-treat eagles, the chiefs switched to more easily obtainable turkey feathers, dyed in a riot of colors. Some of these feathered masterpieces grew to at least five feet long, reaching almost to the ground.

Then, as now, there were grumbles from tribal leaders and his-

This is one of the earliest photos of "Chief" Carl Standingdeer posing with tourists. As you can see, his costume still had a way to go.

torians who wanted to remind everyone that the Cherokees never actually dressed that way and that the ersatz tepees in front of which most of the chiefs posed were another relic of the Western plains and movies rather than the Smokies. However, "Chief" Henry Lambert, whose fifty-five-plus-year stint in the Cherokee tourist wars made him a living legend and sort of elder statesman, put it best: "This isn't history, this is show business, and when you're in show business you have to dress the part." He told the story of how one of his associates bet money that Lambert could make more off tourists if he wore a genuine Cherokee outfit instead of the flashy one. Chief Henry took the bet, left his headdress at home, and spent a day in authentic garb. As he had suspected, the tips he took in were a mere fraction of what he made on a normal day, and he used the Plains version from then on.

Lambert had another experience that proved how much power fiction had over fact. He accompanied the genuine chief of the Cherokees, Walter Jackson, to the Democratic National Convention

These two views of Cherokee's main tourist strip show just how pervasive the image of the Plains Indians became.

"Chief" Ramsey Walkingstick was another of Cherokee's most commonly photographed personalities. Here he seems to be instructing a young princess in the finer arts of pleasing the tourists.

"Chief" Henry Lambert has been posing for tourists' photos for more than fifty years. He says that the more feathers he added to his costume, the more he was called on for photos.

in 1968. As the television news cameras were panning the delegates, the announcer introduced Jackson as the Cherokee nation chief—but the cameras focused on Lambert in his headdress and Indian costume rather than the true chief, who was conservatively attired in a business suit. "I had to talk my way out of that one pretty fast," remembered Lambert.

Chiefing developed its own spin-off industry. Instead of live Indians, some Cherokee entrepreneurs set out black bears that had been shot and stuffed, fiberglass or concrete animals, or simply a tepee with no further encouragement. Tourists would still pay to have their photos taken in such settings. This practice declined as real estate along the busy tourist strip became more prized, and Cherokee leaders have recently sought either to squelch the chiefs' business or to have them present a more historically accurate image.

Inanimate objects such as this deformed dinosaur and stuffed bear (inset) sometimes were placed along the roadside to entice tourists to pay to have their photos taken.

Chief Henry, who was having his photo taken when those same tribal leaders were still papooses, remains philosophical about it all. He plans to continue his work until it is either outlawed or he is too aged to do it any more. "If there's any way of doing it, I don't think I'll let them bury me when I die," he told a reporter in 2005. "I think I'll be skinned and put over a fiberglass frame and just be left sitting there. I really hope somebody will push me inside and out of the rain, though."

People might have gotten their kicks out of crafts and lost a few dollars to the show business Cherokee chiefs, but one does not have to search very far to find the opinion that eating is one of the most important parts of any vacation. Therefore, it should not be sur-

Granny's Restaurant in Sevierville was one of the many that employed stock cartoon hillbilly figures to promote itself.

No other restaurant in the Smokies gloried in the stereotype of the bewhiskered, shiftless hillbilly as much as Wilson's Restaurant in Townsend, Tennessee.

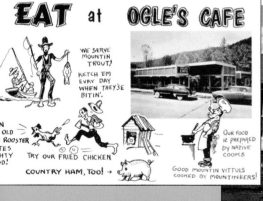

Ogle's Café in Gatlinburg proved it could yuck it up with its own brand of hillbilly humor in this ad.

prising that a wide variety of restaurants sought to silence the growling stomachs of those valued visitors.

Many restaurants tried to come up with some sort of gimmick to help them stand out from the dozens of others lining the same heavily traveled routes. The Cross Ties Restaurant in Pigeon Forge was located near the Goldrush Junction amusement park, about which you will hear much more in chapter 5. The Cross Ties was distinctive because patrons were seated in former railroad dining cars parked on the premises. In Gatlinburg during the 1960s, the Lazy Susan Restaurant advertised itself as a "new concept in dining": customers sat at tables whose tops revolved to deliver the food to each seat. It may have been a new concept in Gatlinburg dining, but apparently it was not successful, because the Lazy Susan is now more like a black-eyed Susan—that is, pushing up daisies.

Speaking of lazy, one way local restaurants strove to get attention was by employing the well-worn stereotype of the bewhiskered, barefoot hillbilly. It might seem odd that such an unflattering image of the mountain country would be so prevalent in its own backyard, but as future chapters will show, business owners in the Smokies seemed to take great pleasure in mining the theme for all it was worth. If the hillbilly image helped sell the product, they were perfectly willing to employ it.

The best example of this line of thinking was Wilson's Hillbilly Restaurant in Townsend. Not only was the stereotype a part of its name, but all of its advertising was built around rural humor. "Recommended by Cousin Clem" was the slogan, even though no one seemed to know just why Clem's endorsement was so special. (Perhaps he was the region's own Duncan Hayseed.) The advertisements promoted the main entrees, "ho-made loaf bred, country ham and fride chicken," and revealed that the owners were "John and Norma Wilson and our Friendly Banker." The restaurant's exterior was adorned with cartoon scenes of hillbilly life that looked somewhat as though the characters in *Li'l Abner* had interbred with those in *Barney Google and Snuffy Smith*.

Not every restaurant went after a certain motif, a la Wilson's and the other hillbilly examples. Buffets and cafeterias seemed especially popular among these more generic entries. Ogle's Café was a landmark, as were the Ogles themselves, who were among the first pioneers to settle in Gatlinburg. The family name remains by far the area's most common. Bunting's Apple Tree Inn did not fall far from its roots in Pigeon Forge. And considering Pigeon Forge's later prominence, it is amusing to see ads such as a 1959 one for Butler's Farm Restaurant that do not even mention the community by name, instead merely stating, "On U.S. 441, five miles north of Gatlinburg."

Speaking of which, in an effort to impress potential visitors, the community issued a press release in the summer of 1968 that crowed, "Still growing today, Pigeon Forge has everything to offer the tourist: 21 fine motels able to accommodate 750, six Grade A restaurants and two drive-in eating establishments, one drugstore with a pharmacist, five groceries, a variety store, dress shop, washerette, car wash, seven gas stations and an endless array of tourist attractions and entertainment." Today, it sometimes seems that approximately the same number of businesses can be found within a one-block area in Pigeon Forge. (At least we know that the economy in Pigeon Forge was booming, as a similar directory from just three years earlier bragged about the community's four restaurants, two drive-ins, and ten motels totaling accommodations for 250.)

If anyone staying in any of the mountain resorts asked "What's for breakfast?" they would have an amazing choice: pancakes, flapjacks, or griddle cakes. Yes, all three were the same, and there is probably nowhere else on the face of the earth with such an enormous concentration of pancake houses in one spot. Repeated at-

"I Cleaned My

Plate

For A Prize!"

at

OGLE'S RESTAURANT

Please present this ticket at desk

The disgruntled tourist who pasted this Ogle's card in his scrapbook groused, "I cleaned my plate, they cleaned my wallet. I didn't get a prize, either."

It was hard to mistake the distinctive shape of this Pigeon Forge pancake house, no matter what name it carried. The view at left shows the restaurant when it was owned by legendary Pigeon Forge businessman Z Buda, whose ventures almost single-handedly defined the town's commercial section in the 1960s.

Pancakes, cartoon bears, and the Smoky Mountains name all came together to make this one of the region's most emblematic signs.

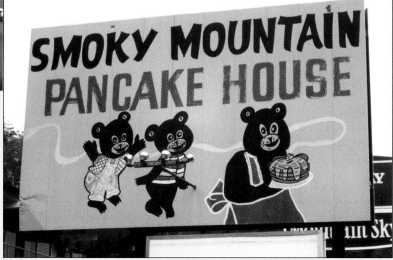

tempts to find out why this is so produced no conclusive answers. The best theory seems to be that pancakes just somehow seem to fit the mountain image of a farmer's wife cooking breakfast over a hearth. Be that as it may, if one were in the mood for pancakes—and one had better be, in Gatlinburg or Pigeon Forge—there was no limit to the variety available.

Many of Pigeon Forge's businesses—restaurants, motels, camp-grounds, and miniature golf courses—were the creations of a local entrepreneur with the undeniably unusual name of Z Buda. Some-what of a shadowy figure to historians, Buda preferred to do much of his philanthropic work from behind a curtain, as it were. His close friends report that many of his businesses were actually the result of him using his own money to open an establishment on behalf of some individual he deemed worthy of a stake. In 2004, shortly before his death, Sevier County's Walters State Community College honored Buda at a ceremony in which the school's gymnasium was named for him.

With so many locally owned examples—not only Z Buda's but everyone else's—from which to choose, it might seem that national restaurant chains would have had little chance to make much of an impression. While that is at least partially true, Howard Johnson's raised its orange roof in Gatlinburg and became a long-standing resident there, with its namesake motel surviving even after the restaurant's demise. Over in Maryville, someone obviously decided that Howard Johnson's orange and teal Simple Simon logo was too good to limit to just one establishment, so that community featured its own Simple Simon Restaurant with a very similar neon depiction of the famous nursery rhyme character on its sign.

Some of the chain restaurants established mountain locations that long outlasted their flatlander cousins. Such was the story of the chain of Lum's restaurants, which originated in Miami and soon had

Howard Johnson's brought its orange roof, blue-green spire, and Simple Simon logo to Gatlinburg in the mid-1960s.

Jack's Hamburgers, a chain based in Birmingham, Alabama, came to Gatlinburg in 1968. As the bottom photo shows, Jack's outdoor dining area faced the infamous Tour through Hell attraction across the street, which must have been an appetizing way to spend a meal.

The Lum's Restaurant outlet in Gatlinburg continued operating for years after the national chain had gone bankrupt.

Kentucky Fried Chicken obviously began nesting in the Smokies years ago. The top photo shows an early usage of the logo and Colonel Sanders at a restaurant/motel complex in Maryville, Tennessee; the bottom photo shows one of the chain's familiar red-and-white striped pagoda buildings from the 1960s, complete with Colonel Sanders weathervane on the peak.

customers nationwide guzzling down its "hot dogs steamed in beer." The name was admittedly—at least in the beginning—lifted from radio's long-running situation comedy serial, *Lum and Abner*, which concerned itself with the misadventures of two rustic storekeepers in Pine Ridge, Arkansas. The radio show was only a memory by the time the Lum's chain began, which is probably why the restaurant's founders thought they needed no permission to use the name.

They discovered that they were wrong when they attempted to start a second chain known as Abner's Beef House. At that point the real Lum and Abner stepped in and put a stop to that. Even though Abner's was put on the chopping block, the Lum's half of the business was allowed to continue operations, inasmuch as it had been in existence for so long with no challenge to its usage of the name.

Like Howard Johnson's and many other older restaurant franchises, Lum's was eventually done in not by its unauthorized name but by the proliferation of fast-food competitors. The chain was officially out of business by the early 1980s, but in small pockets across the country individual owners purchased their locations and continued operating them under the Lum's name. That was the case with the Gatlinburg store, where the owner even took it upon himself to redesign the logo and alter his menu to fit a more updated image. Gone were the hot dogs steamed in beer, and since the owner had no knowledge of the long-ago radio program, he equated the name Lum with "lumberjack," splashing his advertising with a Paul Bunyan lookalike whose type was rarely seen in the Great Smokies.

Plaid-shirted Minnesota lumberjacks may have been scarce in the Tennessee/North Carolina hills, but the same could not be said for bears. From the time visitors first began flocking to the Smokies, the native black bears had been among the most popular sights. The wits behind the Yogi Bear cartoons were not exaggerating when they had Yogi and little buddy Boo Boo express their exasperation with the carloads of tourists who mechanically chanted, "Lookitthebears, lookitthebears, lookitthebears."

This popularity was not lost on business owners, and the hairy plantigrades' legendary appetites made them the perfect emblems for any number of restaurants. A close inspection of the signage for these locales reveals quite a variety of approaches: there were cartoony bears dressed as chefs or waiters, realistic bears that closely resembled their cousins in the wild, and Smokey Bear clones who simply smiled and waved at tourists.

Most of these standard elements could also be found in souvenir shops, which seemed to fall somewhere between being classified with the crafts stores and with the attractions. Pigeon Forge's Three Bears Gift Shop, as one might expect, sported a trio of fiberglass bruins on its marquee. Loudly colored signage proclaimed, "Feed Live Bears!" (I doggies, that's shore a heap more fun than feedin' 'em after they're dead.) Cherokee mined the Plains Indians image for its souvenir shops as much as it did for its handicrafts and chiefs. The Twin Tepees store was hard to miss because of its dual peaks, while the Cherokee Trader featured a neon rendition of a dancing brave. The Big Chief lived up to its name with giant statuary in front representing an oversized Indian with upraised arm in the clichéd "how" greeting.

Then there was Gatlinburg's Rebel Corner, which became an icon of southern roadside kitsch, and that's not just whistlin' "Dixie," brother. Anyone who caught even a glimpse of the Rebel Corner would have known they were not in Chicago or New York. The building was covered with Confederate flags and the shapes of Confederate soldiers in a variety of poses. The selection of souvenirs inside was fairly standard for the era, but somewhat surprisingly, people were not asked to use Confederate money to pay for them. Changing times and political correctness would likely have eventually turned

Bears could take many forms on the roadside signage throughout the mountains, as these two examples show.

Pigeon Forge's Three Bears Gift Shop featured a combination of live bruins and fiberglass replicas.

Souvenirs of the Cherokees could be found at the Tomahawk Gift Shop, Cherokee Trader, and Big Chief Gift Shop, among countless others.

the Rebel Corner into a lost cause, but it met its fate in a great 1992 fire that consumed both the store and its neighbor, Ripley's Believe It or Not! Museum.

Whereas a great revival of interest in all of these types of businesses has occurred in recent years, as far back as 1963, tourist guides were encouraging people to do exactly the sort of documentation that makes books of this type possible today. For example, consider this prophetic paragraph from a list of camera tips published in Chattanooga: "Signs can be used as titles for your slide series or movies. Take pictures of your hotel, motel and restaurant signs; they tell a story in themselves. Photograph city limit signs, street signs, and highway route signs. Best of all, for giant size titles use outdoor advertising posters as backgrounds to tell the story of where you're going!"

By now you are asking whether there was anything for tourists to do in these mountain towns besides take photos, buy candy and crafts, and eat (not the crafts, hopefully). Yes, there was, and we will begin delving into that in our next chapter. Either be prepared to get out your wallet or hold onto it with an iron grip, because we are about to enter the wonderful world of the roadside attraction.

Yankees and other Union
sympathizers had to
beware—and hold onto their
wallets—when they ventured
near Gatlinburg's Rebel Corner.
(Warren Reed Collection)

Greetings from
GATLINBURG

After beginning as a sleepy
mountain community devoted
to native handicrafts, Gatlinburg
had grown into a conglomeration
of attractions, motels, and
restaurants by the 1970s.

THREE

More Fun Than a Monkey
in a Supermarket

No one could accuse the mountain country of being short on entertainment. Whether one were looking for something enlightening or,
conversely, for pure escapism, there were unlimited opportunities for
both.

Falling into the former category were the various outdoor dramas that were part of a fad that swept over the southern states in
the 1950s and 1960s. The South, with its generally fair summer-
time weather and lengthy tourist seasons, may have been a natural whelping spot for this genre. The first of the southern outdoor
dramas is generally conceded to be *The Lost Colony*, which was first
performed in 1940 on North Carolina's Roanoke Island. It remained
alone in its field until after the war years had come and gone.

Around 1948, playwright Kermit Hunter began preparing the
script for a presentation that would cover roughly 250 years of Cherokee Indian history. He worked closely with Harry Davis, longtime
director of *The Lost Colony*, and the two came up with the idea for
what would become the Mountainside Theater in Cherokee, North
Carolina.

The resulting drama was titled *Unto These Hills*, taken from a
quote from Psalm 121, "I will lift up mine eyes unto the hills, from
whence cometh my help." The play had its premiere on July 1, 1950,
and no small part of its success resulted from the fact that the ma-

The Cherokee Historical Association
presents...

Unto These Hills

A Drama of the Cherokee Indian

Nightly except Monday
JUNE 24th at 8 p.m. through AUGUST 31st, 1958
Mountainside Theatre
CHEROKEE, NORTH CAROLINA

56 Kermit Hunter's outdoor drama, *Unto These Hills,* premiered in Cherokee in July 1950, giving tourists a vest-pocket course in the tribe's history.

Two key scenes from *Unto These Hills:* (top) A remarkably well-fed Hernando de Soto passes through Cherokee territory; (bottom) Chief Junaluska saves the life of General Andrew Jackson during the battle of Horseshoe Bend. Junaluska would live to regret that act of heroism.

jority of the performers in it were residents of the reservation, acting out the "true" story of their ancestors.

The incredibly detailed plot began with Hernando de Soto's arrival in Cherokee territory but then skipped ahead to the vast problems that faced the tribe in the 1800s. During the battle of Horseshoe Bend, Cherokee chief Junaluska saved the life of General Andrew Jackson. Jackson repaid the favor when he became president by ordering the removal of all the Cherokees from their ancestral homelands. In the emotional climax, the amphitheater audience could watch as the disheartened Cherokees began their horrific march along the Trail of Tears to their new home in Oklahoma.

A possibly apocryphal story told at the time of Davis's death in 1968 held that during this moving scene, one of the actors would black out his two front teeth and grin moronically at the rest of the cast as soon as the order to march was given, causing his fellow performers to snicker at what was supposed to be the worst moment of their lives. One of Davis's obituaries concluded, "This bothersome habit was broken for good when, during one performance, the young actor turned for his nightly prank and grinned straight into the face of director Davis, appropriately clad and made up as a Cherokee gentleman."

One of the most often-illustrated sequences of the pageant was the spectacular Eagle Dance, performed by athletic young braves clad in outfits that showed how the Cherokees actually used the traditional eagle feathers, in contrast to the Western-style headdresses worn by Chief Henry and his cohorts on the tourist-laden streets. When the photo chiefs were forced to switch from eagle to turkey feathers in 1954, one wonders whether the Eagle Dance had to be changed to the Turkey Trot. No, I guess not.

Kermit Hunter, for his part, did not waste any time once *Unto These Hills* was headed into those hills. For the summer of 1951,

The *Unto These Hills* souvenir program from 1969 was one of the hundreds of promotional pieces to feature the pageant's impressive Eagle Dance.

HORN IN THE WEST

EXCITING OUTDOOR DRAMA ABOUT A THING CALLED FREEDOM

DANIEL BOONE LIVES!
JUNE 23 THRU AUGUST 26, 1972
NIGHTLY EXCEPT MONDAYS
BOONE, NORTH CAROLINA

Kermit Hunter followed up the success of *Unto These Hills* with *Horn in the West,* the life story of Daniel Boone.

During the late 1960s, *Horn in the West* snared big-name talent when Fess Parker, star of NBC-TV's *Daniel Boone* series, re-created his role for several performances. (Hugh Morton Collection)

another of his historical dramas premiered, quite far from the Indian lore of Cherokee in both theme and space. *Horn in the West* was performed in Boone, North Carolina, in the newly constructed Daniel Boone Amphitheater. So, can you guess who was the main subject of the play? (If you said "Davy Crockett," you are hereby requested to turn in your coonskin cap.) Yes, tourists were presented with the life story of Dan'l Boone himself, in company with all of his pioneer friends and enemies.

The fact that *Horn in the West* did not immediately intrude on *Unto These Hills*'s territory no doubt helped both to become institutions in their respective communities. In the mid-1960s, *Horn in the West* scored a coup that even the Cherokees could not boast. Fess Parker, Disney's ex–Davy Crockett who was then starring as Daniel Boone in a successful prime-time NBC television series, was lured to North Carolina to essay the starring role in the play for a few performances. Missing was his bearded humorous TV sidekick Cincinnatus, played on the tube by Dallas McKennon, but one of the play's regular characters, comic relief Rev. Isaiah Sims, ably filled the gap (the Cumberland one, that is).

In many people's minds, Parker had become the embodiment of Boone, just as he had been the living, breathing Davy Crockett a decade earlier. Even historical dramas had to deal with the frequent mixing of fact and fiction that the public had come to expect. Remember in the last chapter when someone bet Chief Henry that he would make more money from his photos if he were dressed in authentic Cherokee garb instead of a Plains Indians costume? *Horn in the West* at one time set out to convince everyone that in real life, Daniel Boone did not wear a cap with a raccoon's tail dangling from the back. That was a lost battle before it began, and Boone's striped headgear was restored to the play—historical inaccuracy and all.

We do not know just how Kermit Hunter reacted to all of this, but he knew when he had a good thing going, and in 1957 he added a third production to his trilogy of the history of the Great Smoky Mountains. Another outdoor amphitheater was built in Gatlinburg to handle Hunter's newest chapter, *Chucky Jack*. Chucky who? Maybe the relative obscurity of its subject matter contributed to this play's mostly forgotten reputation. From the original synopsis, we learn what it was about: "Few casual readers of early American history know of the founding of the State of Franklin, the fourteenth state of the young nation. These early dramatic changes in early government are closely linked with the life of John Sevier. Hero of King's Mountain—one of the first settlers to push down the green valleys to the west—member of the Continental Congress—founder of the Lost State of Franklin—first governor of Tennessee—one of the truly great

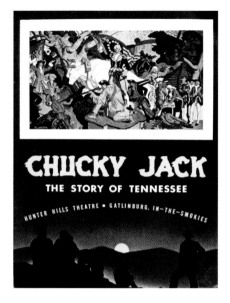

The third leg of Kermit Hunter's Smoky Mountains trilogy of outdoor dramas was *Chucky Jack,* which was not nearly as successful as the first two. (Sevier County Library collection)

American patriots, John Sevier, called by the Indians 'Chucky Jack' from his pioneer home on the Nolichucky River."

John Sevier may have played an important role in Tennessee history—and of course, the county in which Sevierville, Gatlinburg, and Pigeon Forge are situated is named in his honor—but for some reason *Chucky Jack* just never caught on the way Hunter's two previous dramas did. Even the fact that the play's operators had a small tram-type train they called the Chucky Jack Special picking up tourists and tootling them around Gatlinburg did not seem to help. When *Chucky Jack* was finally chucked, the amphitheater was donated to the University of Tennessee and became known as the Hunter Hills Theater.

Not to be discouraged, Hunter plied his trade in other areas of the South and elsewhere. His Civil War musical, *Honey in the Rock*, was performed in Beckley, West Virginia, and he tackled biblical history with his life of St. Paul, *Thy Kingdom Come*, which shared the Daniel Boone Amphitheater with *Horn in the West*. Late in his career, Hunter even penned a sequel to *Unto These Hills*, appropriately known as *Trail of Tears*, to be performed near the terminus of that infamous trail at Tahlequah, Oklahoma. None of these works made the same lasting impression as his original two. Both dramas are still being presented in the summer months today, but *Horn in the West* is the only one that leaves Hunter's original script untouched.

With the season that began in June 2006, *Unto These Hills* was completely rewritten, with the title the only remnant of the 1950 version. The new scriptwriter was Hanay Geiogamah of UCLA, who discarded Hunter's emphasis on the events leading up to the Trail of Tears and chose to make the pageant a celebration of Cherokee culture, music, and dance. Sometimes even presentations that are supposed to be historical can seem a bit outmoded for modern tastes.

History of the nondramatized type was the idea behind Gatlinburg's Homespun Valley Mountaineer Village, opened in 1951 as arguably the town's first true tourist attraction outside of the craft shops and candy stores. Homespun Valley sought to portray the "life of a pioneer," according to its publicity—more specifically, the lifestyle carried on in the Great Smokies before the onslaught of them thar touristers.

Among Homespun Valley's rustic sights was the grinding of corn into cornmeal, which was then packaged and sold in the attraction's general store. The village smithy stood, even if not under a spreading chestnut tree, while every Saturday night featured an old-fashioned barn dance (with the *Grand Ole Opry* playing on the radio in the background, we wonder?). Restored mountain cabins and barns gave the overly citified a view of what mountain living was truly all about.

All of the commercial development around Gatlinburg swallowed up Homespun Valley so gradually that its demise has not even been documented. It was still hanging on in the late 1960s, with a goofily mod rendition of its logo and nightly stage appearances by a male quartet known as the Town Criers. Rather than the fiddle players of old, the Town Criers fell more closely into the mold of clean-cut groups such as the Four Freshmen, the Wellingtons, and the Sandpipers. Apparently not long thereafter, Homespun Valley was finally spun home.

One of the other sights at Homespun Valley was its working moonshine still, whose operators were "makin' a run of corn likker." This was the attraction's nod to the hillbilly culture that many tourists expected to find in any mountain area. As we saw in our discussion of restaurants in the previous chapter, this image has always

FOR FAMILY FUN — VISIT

HOMESPUN VALLEY

Mountaineer Village

WHERE THE PIONEER PAST LIVES AGAIN

Makin' "a run" of corn likker at Homespun Valley

AIRPORT ROAD — CENTER OF TOWN
GATLINBURG, TENN.

Homespun Valley Mountaineer Village is generally acknowledged as Gatlinburg's first attraction not related to handicrafts.

This 1968 ad for Homespun Valley Mountaineer Village looks positively bizarre, with its groovy lettering and the decidedly nonmountaineer appearance of the Town Criers quartet.

occupied a rather unusual position. While many residents despise the stereotypical bearded hillbilly with floppy hat and corncob pipe, sleeping in the yard with rifle, hound dog, and handy jug of corn squeezins, they also knew that trading on such a popular caricature could be an easy—if somewhat guilty—road to riches. In retrospect, it seems an obvious conclusion that the cartoon hillbilly bore as little resemblance to real-life mountain residents as Bugs Bunny did to a real rabbit, so in the end, many were content to play on the image and know that the joke was actually on the tourists who swallowed it.

This brings us to the topic of Pigeon Forge's Hill-Billy Village, a sprawling complex that shuffled into town circa 1954. Although first and foremost a souvenir store, the Hill-Billy Village also borrowed an idea or two from Homespun Valley and displayed confiscated moonshine stills and mountain cabins. One difference between the two attractions' approaches was that Hill-Billy Village was quite open about its debt to the mountain folk of comic strips and animated cartoons: nearly every display was decorated with wooden figures that bore more than a passing resemblance to the characters in *Li'l Abner* and/or *Barney Google and Snuffy Smith*.

Inside the store proper, visitors could watch glassblowers, candle makers, and candy cooks turning out their wares, which were then put up for sale (no big surprise there). Even the building's exterior walls, which faced busy U.S. 441, made no secret of the complex's approach to mountain life, with purposely backward lettering and hillbilly iconography on every conceivable loud yellow surface. Even more amazing is that Hill-Billy Village survives in an almost unchanged form to this day—delighting many, repulsing others, but helpin' separate the tourist folks from some of their greenbacks all the while.

Something of a backwoods mystery surrounds an attraction that opened on May 1, 1968. The Hillbilly Museum in Pigeon Forge sounds as if it were just another name for the exhibits at Hill-Billy Village, but since the two advertised independently of each other, that obviously is not the case. At any rate, we hereby acknowledge the Hillbilly Museum's presumed short-lived existence as (in its own words) "the most educational attraction in the Great Smoky Mountains." A decade earlier, another Pigeon Forge museum with the intriguing name of Arrows to Atoms claimed to "tell the colorful story of the Great Smoky Mountains area from the early Indians to the present. Includ-

Pigeon Forge's Hill-Billy Village employed every known mountaineer stereotype and continues almost unchanged after more than fifty years of operation.

At the Oconaluftee Indian Village in Cherokee, visitors could experience life in an authentic re-creation of a Native American settlement.

ed among the attractive exhibits are pioneer items used by President Andrew Johnson."

The general idea behind such places as the Hillbilly Museum, Arrows to Atoms, and Homespun Valley could also be found with a different flavor over in Cherokee. *Unto These Hills* was one way to expose people to Native American history, but it was, after all, merely a drama presented for spectators. To get the full impact, those attending the spectacle were urged to visit the Oconaluftee Indian Village, in many ways a Cherokee parallel to Homespun Valley. One of its brochures described the sights: "It is a full-size replica of an 18th century Cherokee community brought to life. Indian guides in native costumes will lead you past mud huts and primitive cabins and rustic arbors in which Indians are making dug-out canoes with fire and ax, stringing beads, molding ropes of clay into pots, weaving baskets and finger-weaving cloth."

Oconaluftee and *Unto These Hills* shared ownership by the Cherokee Historical Association, with a third project of the organization being the Museum of the Cherokee Indian. From the outside, this building looked very little like a tourist attraction, with a dignified finish and elegant stained glass windows depicting various heroes of Cherokee history. Inside, the displays presented sights that could not easily be duplicated in person at Oconaluftee, and between the three arms of the historical association, tourists received a good (though not necessarily always accurate) lesson in Cherokee culture.

Cherokee history also received commercial exploitation in the form of the Cyclorama of the Cherokee Indian. It covered many of the same events and personages as the similarly named museum but did so somewhat more crudely. Mannequins acted out the story of Cherokee life and the Trail of Tears under black light, which made them look more like escapees from a theme park dark ride.

Over in Gatlinburg, where the Cherokee aspect of history was mostly all but ignored, one could nevertheless find the Cherokee-Rama. Like other attractions located near famous battlefields, such as Horseshoe Bend, Alabama, and Lookout Mountain, Tennessee, the Cherokee-Rama used a miniaturized table-top landscape to act out its version of history with tiny animated figures. This is likely the same attraction that by 1968 was known as the Trail of Tears, where "a thousand miniature figures tell colorfully, with flashing lights and smoking guns, the exciting, historic story of the Cherokee Indians." It has been said that no one can go broke underestimating the taste of the public, but the fact is that both the Cyclorama and Cherokee-Rama went to the happy hunting grounds years ago, leaving their more realistic companions standing tall.

Lest we forget, not every attraction in the hill country was built around hillbillies or Indians. The region was well known for its strong religious roots, and the Bible Belt sure didn't buckle when it came time to merge that tradition with the tourism industry.

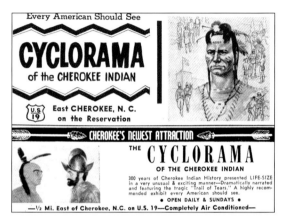

The Cyclorama of the Cherokee Indian presented history in a rather lurid fashion. In the bottom ad, a Cherokee chief and Hernando de Soto hold a staring contest to decide who will rule the Land of the Smokies.

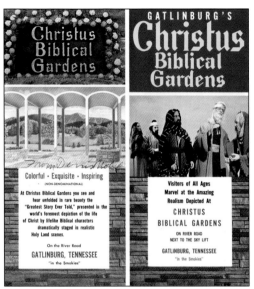

These are two of the earliest brochures for Gatlinburg's serene Christus Biblical Gardens, today known as Christus Gardens.

Given this heritage, it is somewhat surprising that the tourism business waited so long to take sanctuary in the realm of religion. The story began halfway across the state from the Smokies, when Ronald S. Ligon, a sophomore at Vanderbilt University at Nashville, contracted a severe case of tuberculosis. His official biography described how this seeming tragedy would come to have a greater purpose: "It was during the period of deepest depression that Ligon resolved, at first secretly, that should his health be restored, he would devote whatever time and efforts it required to build some type of significant memorial to express permanently his gratefulness to divine providence."

Ligon indeed recovered from his illness, and while tending to the business of life, the idea of his memorial was never far from his mind. Ligon reportedly racked up some eighty thousand frequent-flyer miles by frequently flying to far-flung places around the globe, examining previous religious memorials. During a visit to a wax museum near Niagara Falls, Ligon first became aware of the startling realism that could be produced by that medium. Slowly the idea dawned that his memorial could somehow incorporate wax figures.

He still had no definite location for his masterpiece, but that changed when he first visited Gatlinburg with the more prosaic intention of either buying a motel or building one from the ground up. When a real estate agent showed Ligon a vacant piece of property on that town's River Road, backed up against the hulk of Crockett Mountain, the would-be memorial maker saw that this was the perfect spot for his long-unrealized vision.

Ligon had previously struck up a friendship with Stanley and Derek Deroy and their families, the creative geniuses behind the Niagara Falls museum he had enjoyed so much. Now that he had a place to call his own, Ligon put the Deroys into overdrive to design realistic wax re-creations of scenes from the life of Christ. Derek Deroy prepared concept art from Ligon's mental visualization of each tableau, and a London company, Gems Ltd., was enlisted to create life-size wax figures.

August 13, 1960, was set for the opening of the Christus Biblical Gardens. As that date approached and Gatlinburg made great preparations to welcome its newest attraction, one little problem cropped up—all of the wax figures had arrived and been installed except the ones representing Christ and the two thieves that would hang in the Crucifixion scene. Such an omission was sure to be noticed by even those who were not Bible scholars. The trio of wax men was hurriedly shipped from London to Baltimore, where they were picked up by private plane and flown to Knoxville, touching the ground at 1:30 A.M. on opening day. The drive to Gatlinburg took until 3:00 A.M., leaving a scant six hours to complete the scene before the first visitors entered the room. Yes, they made it—just another seemingly miraculous event in the attraction's history.

Christus Gardens, as the name was eventually condensed, has remained one of Gatlinburg's leading attractions, but its somewhat fragile displays tend to require considerably more care than, say, the concrete dinosaurs of a miniature golf course. To that end, in recent years Christus Gardens has been fortunate to obtain the services of Mark Pedro, whose love for the displays and their subject matter rivals that of Ligon himself. Pedro has expanded and elaborated on the Deroys' original designs. For example, the Nativity diorama lacked a figure of the infant Jesus; for at least forty years, his presence was suggested only by a glow coming from the manger. Through Pedro's

For years, Christus Garden's opening Nativity scene did not actually feature the figure of the infant Jesus, but only a glow emanating from the manger.

efforts, Christus Gardens's Nativity scene has now been brought in line with the millions of other renditions seen around the world during the Christmas season. With the closing of many wax museums in tourist centers across the nation, Pedro has also obtained additional figures. He chuckles about the fact that visitors do not realize that some of the biblical personages started their wax lives as Leonardo da Vinci or Spanish conquistadors of the Hernando de Soto variety. With the proper makeup and hairstyle, they all blend together into a harmonious whole.

In the tourism world, it may be true that imitation is the sincerest form of flattery—but it is more likely related to the famous quote from Red Skelton, "Imitation is *not* the sincerest form of flattery; it's plagiarism." When imitators begin popping up in an attraction's

VISIT GATLINBURG'S TOUR THRU HELL . . .

- See the Lake of Fire.
- See a replica of the Coin Judas received for betraying Christ.
- Walk on the Burning Brimstone.
- See the Invisible Hand with the drop of water floating thru the air.
- See Pontius Pilate's hands turn to blood before your very eyes.
- See the Wicked Jezebel and many other attractions.

In 1968, Gatlinburg's Tour through Hell presented a different view of the Bible from that seen at Christus Gardens—and the attraction soon went straight to its namesake geographic location.

immediate neighborhood, it is a good sign that some enterprising individual has decided to try to tap into the same market. Be that as it may, Christus Gardens probably did not feel flattered in the least when, around 1968, someone brought another biblical-themed attraction to Gatlinburg—the infamous Tour through Hell.

Yes, you read that correctly. Some vacations might have seemed to originate in the Bad Place, but the Tour through Hell attempted to send its visitors there in person. In stark contrast to Christus Gardens, which was never backward about telling Ligon's inspiring life story, the mastermind behind the Tour through Hell was identified only as the "Chaplain." Housed in a building that looked vaguely like a cave, with twin volcanoes spouting smoke, the Tour through Hell featured a variety of gruesome displays that stemmed from the opposite side of the Bible from Christus Garden's scenes. According to the attraction's only known press release, "You will thrill at the many interesting things to be seen, such as the Lake of Fire and Pontius Pilate's hands turning to blood before your very eyes. You'll actually walk on the burning brimstone. You'll actually see an invisible hand with the drop of water floating in the air, which the rich man in the 16th chapter of Luke prayed for."

No one has yet answered the question of how anyone could see

Fields of the Wood, near Murphy, North Carolina, re-created religious sites and icons including this gigantic Ten Commandments that occupied an entire hillside.

a hand if it were invisible, and many other questions about the Tour through Hell also remain unanswered. It appears that tourists generally decided that not only wouldn't they want to live there, but hell also was not even a nice place to visit. All traces of the brimstone burg disappeared years ago, although across the country, some of its elements have survived in local churches' "Judgment Houses" that appear each Halloween. Like the demons it hosted, the concept apparently has never died completely.

Meanwhile, down in Murphy, North Carolina, the Church of God of Prophecy opened a religious park that owed nothing to anything in Gatlinburg. Fields of the Wood was as much a religious retreat as a true roadside attraction, but it promoted itself right alongside all of its more commercial brethren. Among many other displays, the centerpiece was a replica of the Ten Commandments that covered an entire mountainside, with letters five feet tall and four feet wide. Its low-key approach to tourists must have worked in its favor, because Fields of the Wood still pulls them in today.

Surprising as it may seem, none of these attractions featured its own version of Noah's ark. However, if tourists wanted to see real-life birds and beasts traveling in more than two by two, there were plenty of other opportunities. One of the earliest was Pigeon Forge's Fort Weare Game Park, which modestly advertised with such unassuming terminology as "Exciting—Educational," "Exotic Animal Wonderland," and "The Largest Privately Owned Collection of Zoological Animals in the South." Great jumping kangaroos, who could resist?

Animal attractions generally fell into three different categories: traditional zoos, in which the animals were caged and stared balefully at their visitors; petting zoos, which allowed tourists to intermingle with the critters and feed them; and shows featuring performing varmints of one breed or another. Fort Weare decided to hedge its bets by presenting all three types in a single location. And as if that were not enough to drag in the visitors, it also displayed pioneer relics of the mountain country and Indian crafts made across the mountains in Cherokee. Before its demise, the name was changed to Jungle Cargo, which made even less sense and certainly did not help to haul in more visitors.

It is somewhat ironic that Fort Weare and its live animals were eventually replaced on the same piece of property by the Magic World theme park and its collection of concrete dinosaurs, about which more will be discussed in the next chapter. Long after Fort Weare's retreat, someone else apparently decided to take up its fallen banner with another Pigeon Forge park known as Baby Animal Kingdom, which carried on the petting zoo tradition. Near Chattanooga, the Georgia Game Park went in a different direction with lurid

Animal attractions in the Smokies got their start at the Fort Weare Game Park in Pigeon Forge during the 1950s.

In the days before animal welfare was such a hot topic, roadside zoos such as these thrived. Clark Byers, the sign painter responsible for thirty years of Rock City barn roofs, operated the Georgia Game Park.

MAGGIE ZOO and REPTILE FARM
Featuring animals and reptiles from both the Americas.
Rattlesnakes milked for venom.
CENTER OF MAGGIE, N. C.   OPEN MAY THRU OCTOBER
Larry Mathis, Owner & Operator

GEORGIA GAME PARK
—ON U.S. HIGHWAY 11, 25 MI. SOUTH OF CHATTANOOGA AT RISING FAWN, GA.—

FREAK ANIMALS
WILD ANIMALS
LIONS, BEARS, ETC.

SHELL PRODUCTS
FREE SOUVENIR WITH
EACH GAS FILL UP

2 LARGE SOUVENIR SHOPS
CHENILLE BEDSPREADS
CIDER BAR
FRIED MARBLES
FILM (3 ROLLS $1.00)

billboards that screamed, "See the six-legged dog" and "See the two-headed snake." Yes, there were animals awhile along the hill country highways, whether they made one want to pet them or put them out of their misery.

Other "live animal" attractions make the mind reel, seeming totally, completely out of place in the hills of the Great Smokies. One of the strangest of these was Porpoise Island, which might have looked at home in Miami or St. Augustine or Panama City Beach, Florida, but in Pigeon Forge seemed just plain bizarre. Let's face it: In the mountains, tourists expected to see hillbillies, Indians, and black bears but not Polynesian hula dancers sharing the stage with tropical birds and performing porpoises. Porpoise Island's advertising proclaimed,

"Visit Hawaii without ever leaving the Great Smokies," leaving all logical questions unanswered as to just what those two geographic locations had to do with each other. Porpoise Island was swimming in deep waters and soon sank beneath the salty and smoky waves. (Is that a suitably mixed metaphor for this even more mixed-up attraction?)

Porpoise Island might have seemed to be an anomaly, but believe it or not—no, wait, that was another attraction we'll be getting to later—it was not alone in its quest to bring Florida to Tennessee, or something like that. For a while, other saltwater-taffy-flavored attractions called Mountain Ocean and the Tennessee Porpoise Circus operated nearby, without any greater success.

Ripping off Florida took on an even greater scale when the Tommy Bartlett Water Circus came to Pigeon Forge in 1978. Bartlett, a former CBS-TV and radio celebrity, was a tourism mogul in the Wisconsin Dells who had invaded the South with a deer ranch at Florida's Silver Springs. His Pigeon Forge park was almost a clone of what he had been doing in the Dells, which itself looked like it borrowed a page or several from Florida's famed Cypress Gardens.

Bartlett's Tennessee rendition of his Water Circus survived only as long as the early 1980s. Besides its daring exhibitions of waterskiing, the shows featured the comedy of Dieter Tasso, who demonstrated his juggling ability—though not while on water skis. Also highlighted was a troupe known as the Nomura-Fraire Tahitian Drum Dancers. With Bartlett's show and the antics at Porpoise Island running simultaneously, it is probably safe to say that at no other point did Polynesian acts find so much competition for their skills in the Smoky Mountains.

How did photos from Florida get into this discussion? No, it isn't Florida but Pigeon Forge's Porpoise Island of the 1970s. This attraction somehow just did not seem to fit the hill country image.

Water-skiers and bikini-clad beauties might have been well and fine for Florida and Wisconsin, but their careers in Pigeon Forge were as brief as their swimsuits.

Despite Bartlett's best efforts and a slick ad campaign that made other attractions' publicity look shabby, the Water Circus was just too at odds with the area's normal clientele. Most tourists who visited the Great Smoky Mountains National Park did not come specifically to see lean, athletic young beauties performing in itty-bitty bikinis, so before long, the Bartlett encampment packed up and returned to Wisconsin, where his shows remain a fixture.

The final class of attraction we shall examine in this chapter concerned itself with various modes of transportation. The original amusement in this arena was Gatlinburg's Sky Lift, which rose to the top of the pile in 1954. The Sky Lift exemplified a philosophy that would be repeated in the tourist industry over and over again—namely, that an attraction did not necessarily have to be unique as long as it was in a place where visitors did not expect to find it.

The Sky Lift was a chairlift like those found at ski resorts. The fact that it was not there for the use of skiers but departed from Gatlinburg to take tourists up the side of Crockett Mountain for a Davy's eye view of the greenest state in the land

Gatlinburg's Sky Lift began hauling tourists to the top of Crockett Mountain in 1954 and is still giving them a lift today.

of the free was what made it novel. (In later years, assorted theme parks and other attractions would latch onto the idea with skyrides that transported guests through space in enclosed buckets.) Apparently even the Gatlinburg Sky Lift had enough novelty value to give it sticking power, because it is still there today and just as low-tech as ever. That is comforting to know.

For those who wanted an aerial view of Gatlinburg and the surrounding countryside without trusting life and limb to some swinging chairs, the 342-foot-tall Space Needle opened in May 1970. Like the aforementioned skyrides, observation towers were another craze

The Space Needle opened in Gatlinburg in 1970. At its base are the infamous Rebel Corner souvenir shop and the Parkway Cafeteria, one of dozens of such eating establishments in the area.

in tourist capitals, although they could take many different geometric forms. The Gatlinburg tower's design was less spacey than, say, the one in Panama City Beach, Florida, but it served the same basic purpose of giving tourists the opportunity to look down on everyone else.

In the mid-1970s, another sort of ride to the mountaintop came to town, but with a completely different flavor than the dangly old Sky Lift. The Gatlinburg Aerial Tramway carried guests up to the area's ski resort and ice skating rink atop Mt. Harrison, to the tune of 120 tourists at a whack comfortably ensconced in its cabin. Ski resorts, especially in the southern states, had a disadvantage over other attractions in that they could operate only during very specific times of the year—namely, either when there was snow or when it was cold enough for them to make their own white stuff. By 1977, the area at the top of the Aerial Tramway had solved this problem by throwing its Tyrolean hat into the ring and developing Ober Gatlinburg, a German-themed complex that featured enough oom-pah-pah music and imported beer to make anyone lonely for lederhosen. However, once again proving that there is generally room for just about everyone in Smokies tourism, the tramway and the older Sky Lift continue to co-exist peacefully to this day.

Other transportation-related attractions display antique cars and other vehicles. Like Porpoise Island and the Tommy Bartlett show, this genre was another import from Florida, which had several such attractions. Unlike those other tropical transplants, this concept did not look nearly so out of place, so these automobile-themed exhibits seem to have found a permanent parking place in the hills.

The Smoky Mountain Car Museum in Pigeon Forge dates to 1956, although many of its most promoted exhibits were not added until they became famous—or in some cases, infamous—years later. This museum's collection ranges from the fictional, such as vehicles used

Displays of antique and otherwise notable automobiles first came to the Smokies in the 1950s with these two museums.

By the twenty-first century, the small car museums had morphed into Star Cars, a gigantic exhibition of famous vehicles from movies and television.

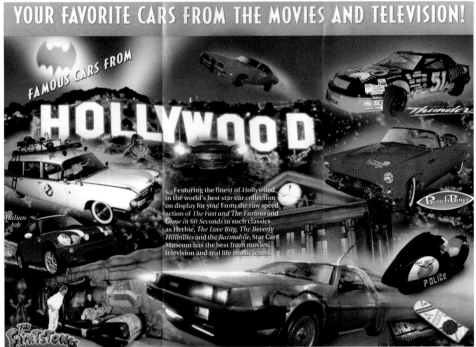

in the James Bond movies, to the all-too-real, including the Cadillac owned by murdered *Grand Ole Opry* and *Hee Haw* comic David "String-bean" Akeman and an unmarked patrol car used by real-life sheriff Buford Pusser. (No screenwriter could have ever concocted a name as colorful as that one.) Competition arose in Gatlinburg from Cox's Antique Car Museum, located near the Mountain View Hotel. It followed the Florida format faithfully, greatly resembling the Carriage Cavalcade at Silver Springs and Horn's Cars of Yesterday at Sarasota.

Many attraction types seem to have exhausted themselves over the years, but the automotive displays continue to breed to this day. In 1997, the Star Cars Museum opened in Gatlinburg to display the eclectic collection of custom cars designed for movies and television by George Barris. Alongside the Batmobile and the souped-up hearse from *The Munsters* was one of the Dodge Chargers not wrecked during the course of the *Dukes of Hazzard* TV series. And, as if seeing one General Lee were not enough—it was probably too much for the more sophisticated crowd—*Hazzard* cast member Ben "Cooter" Jones opened the Cooter's Place museum across the street from the former Jolly Golf course. Jones's connection to the show gave him an inside track when it came to loading up on genuine memorabilia, and even miserly Boss Hogg would have been pleased with the publicity boost it received from the release of the *Hazzard* feature film in 2005. Yee-haw, anyone?

Fairyland was most likely the first attraction in the Pigeon Forge/Gatlinburg area to be aimed squarely at the new baby boomer population.

Fabulous Fairyland

FOR CHILDREN

Robin Hood watches as the Cat Plays the Fiddle for Little Miss Muffet and Little Boy Blue

Most Beautiful Show For Children In The Mountains

ON U. S. HIGHWAY 441 IN
PIGEON FORGE, TENNESSEE
Five Miles North of Gatlinburg

FOUR

Cuttin' Up with the Little Shavers

Nostalgic author Susan Waggoner hit the bull's-eye when she wrote, "To anyone who wasn't part of the baby boom generation, it's almost impossible to convey the sheer pleasure of finding yourself in the center of a world in which you were, well, the center of the world." Waggoner knew this from personal experience, and so do millions of other ex-children who grew up in the 1950s and 1960s. Seemingly every facet of life, from television to toys to food products, was aimed squarely at that ever-growing segment of the population. Tourism was no different, and while earlier attractions could take or leave kids, the tourist destinations that sprang up beginning in the early 1950s preferred to take them—and in the process, to take their doting dads and motherly moms for all they had.

One of the earliest Smokies attractions to aim squarely at the baby boomers was Pigeon Forge's Fairyland (also known in its advertising as Fabulous Fairyland, although whether that was an official part of the name or simply an adjective was not made clear). For the majority of its existence, Fairyland was a project of the Swan family of Knoxville, which had made its dough in the bakery business. Around 1958, Margaret Swan purchased the attraction from its original owner, whose identity has now been lost to history.

Visitors to Fairyland traveled a prescribed route and viewed assorted scenes through windows. The various tableaux were populated by animated figures of the type most often found in department store windows at Christmastime; members of the Swan family recall that most of them were manufactured by a Chicago firm that specialized in such displays. Fairyland's novel approach to this evergreen theme was not to present a single scene from an established story but to intermingle the characters indiscriminately to create some rather odd juxtapositions. According to Fairyland's promotional brochure,

> Little Red Riding Hood and the Wolf are at the entrance to welcome you. Mickey Mouse shows you the way to the show. All Fairyland opens up for you. Robin Hood looks on while the Cat plays the fiddle and Little Bo-Peep and Little Boy Blue dance. The Fairyland Band welcomes you. Wee Willie Winkie comes out of his little house to wake Fairyland up. Simple Simon shrugs as the Pieman shows him his wares.
>
> Then there are the three beautiful panoramas with twelve figures in each one. There is the "Littlest Angel" before the court, learning to fly and giving his toys to the holy infant. You will thrill over going to Grandfather's house for Christmas. From the family in the sleigh, decorating the church, singing carols, baking the goodies, going to bed and even seeing the animals get ready for Christmas. Then Santa fills the stockings and the old goats get ready too.
>
> Lovely Cinderella scrubs and cleans as the invitation comes to the ball. She helps dress the ugly stepsisters and finally the Fairy Godmother turns the mice to a beautiful carriage and Cinderella goes to the ball. See Mickey Mouse's Club House with Mickey, Minnie, Goofy and Donald Duck. The Old Rabbit tries to get the hens to lay the eggs for Easter. After Willie awakens all Fairyland, he nods his head and goes happily to sleep.

These two scenes demonstrate how Fairyland freely mixed and matched the characters from unrelated stories and nursery rhymes. In the top photo, Wee Willie Winkie awakens Goldilocks so she can face the Three Bears; at bottom, Mother Goose and Bobby Shaftoe run a candy store with Little Miss Muffet and Little Boy Blue as customers.

Now, how's *that* for a mixed storybook? Obviously no one from the Disney Studios ever visited Pigeon Forge to catch their star characters moonlighting in Fairyland, but it would not have made much difference in the long run. While Fairyland was still playing out its charming tales in the mid-1970s, it vanished back over the rainbow some time before the end of the decade. Most of the figures reportedly took up residence in a department store in Chattanooga, but their trail grows cold there. The next time you visit Pigeon Forge, stop in at the Ponderosa Restaurant and you might hear the faint giggling of the long-gone folktale folks—the restaurant sits on their former turf.

While Santa Claus was filling stockings in one of the scenes at Fairyland, he was also welcoming youngsters to his own domain across the mountains, Santa's Land in Cherokee. (Not much of a trick for a guy who can be in six different department stores in the same city at once, right?) Although many people have commented on how displaced Jolly Old St. Nick and his cohorts looked when surrounded by mountains, bears, and Indians, the fact is that Santa's Land was hardly unique in its choice of theme.

The post–World War II years brought a sack full of Santa attractions to many different parts of the country. The biggest difference was that most of them grew out of the names of their locales—North Pole, New York, and Santa Claus, Indiana, to name two prime examples. Why did Cherokee become one of Santa's summer homes? No one seems to be able to answer that question, and of all the many attractions discussed in this book, Santa's Land is the most icy when it comes to granting requests for information. Perhaps the *real* Santa hangs out there and is fiercely protecting his trade secrets.

Should this be the case, Santa is operating under the alias of the Lyons family, which opened the snow-filled summer park in 1966. At that time, Santa's Land was basically a small collection of buildings along a meandering pathway, augmented with concrete renditions of the famed nine reindeer and a large Nativity scene to give some balance between the sacred and secular sides of the holiday season. A few live cedar trees were decorated with large ornaments, which probably did not hold up well after being exposed to the outdoor elements for several months.

Over the years, as families came to expect more of a theme park environment from their vacation stops, Santa's Land added features until the original attraction was only a tiny corner of the complex. Petting zoos and amusement rides filled in the gaps, as well as authentic mountain relics such as a gristmill and genuine still (putting Santa right back into Hill-Billy Village territory again). There was even a lake with paddleboat rides and a ride known as the Rudi-Coaster because of the lead car's uncanny resemblance to the most famous reindeer of all. Santa's Land still gives out jollies today—unless one happens to be interested in delving into its history, in which case a lump of coal is about all that can be expected.

(An interesting sidelight is that on the Tennessee side of the hills, Santa and his helpers also hang out year round but do so in shops rather than an amusement park. Beginning with a single Christmas shop in Gatlinburg, the concept expanded until the Sevierville–Pigeon Forge strip is now home to gigantic stores geared toward making everyone feel like Christmas in July—or April or October or whenever they happen to be there.)

The additions during the Santa's Land expansions included a series of giant concrete figures to be used as photo ops. There was a humongous snowman that would have made Frosty tremble in his magic silk hat and an undeniably cranky-looking rabbit that resembled Bugs Bunny on one of his bad days. Considering these giant figures and the preponderance of other amusements in the park, it is somewhat surprising that Santa's Land lacked a miniature golf course. Not to worry—that tourism staple was more than well represented in the rest of the region.

As will be discussed again in chapter 7, miniature golf was itself

PARK AND ZOO
CHEROKEE N.C.

santa's land
CHEROKEE, N.C.
HOME OF
SANTA
AND HIS
HELPERS

Many people have commented that Santa and his staff looked rather out of place in Cherokee, North Carolina, but diligent research has failed to disclose the reason jolly old St. Nick ended up there in the first place.

It is easy to assume that these types of Christmas tree ornaments did not last long when exposed to the weather.

ABOVE: When Santa's Land first opened in 1966, the entrance was denoted by the huge two-dimensional Claus in the top photo; by 1985, he had been replaced by the waving figure shown at bottom.

LEFT: There was no war between the secular and sacred sides of Christmas at Santa's Land, where this Nativity scene and chapel shared space with snowmen and reindeer.

Furniture store owner and frustrated artist Jim Sidwell began constructing dinosaur statues at his home in Murfreesboro, Tennessee, before getting into the miniature golf business.

a product of the South's mountain country. Future Rock City founder Garnet Carter opened what is generally acknowledged as the first true present-day miniature golf course on Lookout Mountain in 1927. However, in most tourist areas of the South, courses took their cue from what might be termed the Gulf Coast style of miniature golf, which involved huge animated statues of dinosaurs and other oversized objects that served as obstacles in the game.

The undisputed leader in this parade was Goofy Golf, founded by Lee Koplin, which spread rapidly along the coast until it reached its peak with the lavish Panama City Beach course in 1959. This operation was the inspiration for Gatlinburg's entry into the larger-than-life game, courtesy of an enterprising businessman, Jim Sidwell.

Sidwell was the traditional frustrated artist, successful in his family's furniture business in Murfreesboro but aching for an outlet for his creativity. When his son, Jim Jr., was old enough to appreciate it, Dad fashioned a dinosaur out of wood and wire mesh as an oversized backyard toy, but a family trip to Panama City Beach during the early 1960s sent Sidwell down a different sort of prehistoric path. "My dad met with Lee Koplin and they started talking about building dinosaurs," Jim Jr. recalled. "Mr. Koplin encouraged my dad to start building miniature golf courses of his own."

Sidwell got down to work with a will, and his Jolly Golf opened in Gatlinburg in 1961. While dinosaurs were the main feature of the course, Sidwell let his imagination run wild—in true Goofy Golf fashion—and included other giant creatures such as a not-so-ferocious gorilla, "Old Pokey Bear," a hollowed-out jack-o'-lantern, and a towering praying mantis that became a standard fixture of many of his future projects. Not limiting himself to the mountains, Sidwell opened Holiday Golf in Daytona Beach in 1962, using many of the same figure designs, and other Jolly Golfs puttered their way into Marietta, Georgia, and Lake of the Ozarks, Missouri.

When it looked like big brontos were going to mean big business, Sidwell came up with a more time-effective way to create his monsters. Rather than the handcrafted wood/mesh method he had used at Jolly Golf and Holiday Golf, he developed molds that allowed the beasts to be mass-produced in fiberglass. With a true dinosaur factory operating out of Murfreesboro, Sidwell supplied saurians to prehistoric-themed parks in Wisconsin and Ohio and to Dinosaur Land in Virginia, among other places across the country. He itched for his own theme park, and we will scratch more than the surface of that in just a moment.

Meanwhile, other miniature golf courses were growing up in the area, although initially not always in the same goofy and jolly form as the Sidwell style. Hillbilly Golf opened in Gatlinburg in 1971, with the novelty of having visitors ride an incline railway from street level to the course's location atop a high bluff. The Putt-Putt Golf course chain, which disdained tricky gimmicks of the dinosaur and windmill variety, set up its orange and white fences around property in both Gatlinburg and Cherokee. Scores of smaller, independently run courses sprouted along the roadsides, some lasting for only a few years and others surviving to become local institutions—and frequently, picturesque ruins today.

Whereas Jolly Golf had originated in a meeting between Sidwell and Koplin, the Goofy Golf in Panama City Beach had been the inspiration for another chain of southern courses. Goony Golf (later

While designing Jolly Golf in Gatlinburg, Jim Sidwell let his imagination run wild and created many different types of giant figures to serve as obstacles in his game.

Hillbilly Golf opened in Gatlinburg in July 1971. It was unique in that players had to ride an incline railway up to the course.

changed to Sir Goony Golf, probably in an attempt to sound less imitative), came to life in Chattanooga in 1960. The course supposedly began with an unidentified individual who sat in the Goofy Golf parking lot with a pad of paper sketching the course's figures. Many of the obstacles at Goony Golf unquestionably had more than a passing resemblance to the Koplin creations.

Goony Golf began franchising itself in 1964, and according to the company's Web site, eventually numbered some thirty-five courses nationwide, probably leading some latter-day beach visitors to surmise that Goofy Golf was the imitator. In the hill country, the original Goony Golf survives on Brainerd Road in Chattanooga, although in 1978 it had to be moved a block from its first location to make way for a shopping center. A Goony Golf reportedly still exists in Knoxville as well.

Goony Golf—later known as Sir Goony Golf—was one of the most widely franchised of the concrete dinosaur genre.

These photos were taken in 1978, when Chattanooga's Goony Golf course was being moved about a block from its original site.

Jim Sidwell's family continues in the miniature golf business today with its chain of Adventure Golf courses.

The tourism boom that hit Pigeon Forge in the 1980s brought forth more miniature golf courses within the space of a couple of miles than could have been found in the whole of the Smokies twenty years earlier. Some of these were even latter-day Sidwell enterprises, such as Adventure Golf, whose trademark was its giant octopus with sprawling tentacles. Variations such as Safari Golf (with pink elephants, yet) and Smoky Bear Golf kept the Sidwell courses company.

At the entrance to Dollywood, a small course tried to make a hole in one for years, under wildly varying themes. Originally known as Bunny-Land Mini Golf, it offered the novelty of wending one's way through cages full of live rabbits. That idea failing, the bunnies were given the boot and it became Nightmare Mini-Golf, with a more foreboding appearance. No one wanted to be welcomed to that nightmare, either. Through all of its forms, this course of many colors was fronted by a giant Gabby Hayes–type Western figure that had formerly manned the buckboard at a defunct chain of hamburger restaurants known as Wagon Ho.

This former chuck wagon driver from the defunct Wagon Ho hamburger chain has stood guard over a Pigeon Forge miniature golf course through several name and theme changes.

More recent miniature golf courses, such as Fantasy Golf in Pigeon Forge, show that old-time creativity and flights of fancy are not relegated to the past.

Fantasy Golf was another of the arrivals of the early 1980s, but in its original form it had little to make it stand out from the rest. After being revamped by Ross and Jo Ogle and their daughter and son-in-law, Brenda and Cary Dodgin, Fantasy Golf became more of a road-side spectacle, with giant fiberglass renditions of dragons, ogres, and other mythological figures.

As with much of the tourism industry, individuality eventually gave way to corporate culture. The Sidwells sold Jolly Golf in the 1990s, and the new owners removed all of the figures except the prehistoric ones, changing the name to Dinosaur Golf. By 2005, that format had been absorbed by the Ripley organization, which built the elaborate Davy Crockett Mini-Golf on the property. In Sevierville, Ripley's was also responsible for Old MacDonald's Farm Mini-Golf, possibly the most elaborate course ever built in that part of the country. The Ripley courses depended heavily on their own style of fiber-glass figures, achieving effects that could never have been created in the wood-and-mesh medium. When Dinosaur Golf became extinct, however, the Sidwells removed and preserved the figures that were still in reasonably good condition, and at last report they were being transferred to new stomping grounds in Branson, Missouri.

Now, what about Sidwell's desire to have a park of his own? City records show that in 1970, Sidwell received a permit to build a miniature golf course in Pigeon Forge. The piece of property he used had formerly been home to the Fort Weare Game Park: it would now trade live animals for the fiberglass variety. Soon, however, Sidwell's unfettered imagination outgrew his plans for yet another Jolly Golf–style course.

Whereas Jolly Golf and its kin had been inspired and encouraged by the Gulf Coast's Goofy Golf, Sidwell may have taken time to do some further research during trips to Florida's Miracle Strip. Jungle Land, a creation of tourism legend Val Valentine—who would come

This miniature golf course in Cherokee carries on the grand tradition of mixing Plains Indian iconography with the natural beauty of the reservation.

to the Smokies himself in future years—was housed in a towering concrete volcano. Visitors could roam the passageways and see sights meant to evoke the ambiance of the South Seas. Whether this was the direct inspiration or not, Sidwell had soon enlarged his Pigeon Forge golf course with a huge volcano, which offered paying guests a rather lengthy funhouse-type stroll. The name he chose for his new complex was Magic World.

The Volcano Walk at first was Magic World's main feature. In a series of grottoes, visitors viewed scenes that were alternately eerie and humorous. The Abominable Snowman lurked in one cavern, while in another could be seen—or could *not* be seen, as the case may be—the Invisible Man, whose glowing hat and animated gloves provided the only evidence of his existence. At another point, a skeleton could be glimpsed on the floor while its semi-transparent spirit, a bewhiskered old gold miner, chipped away at the wall. (We suppose you'd call that figure a "pros-specter.")

OVERLEAF: This is one of the earliest maps of Jim Sidwell's Magic World complex in Pigeon Forge, where dinosaurs and volcanoes ruled the earth.

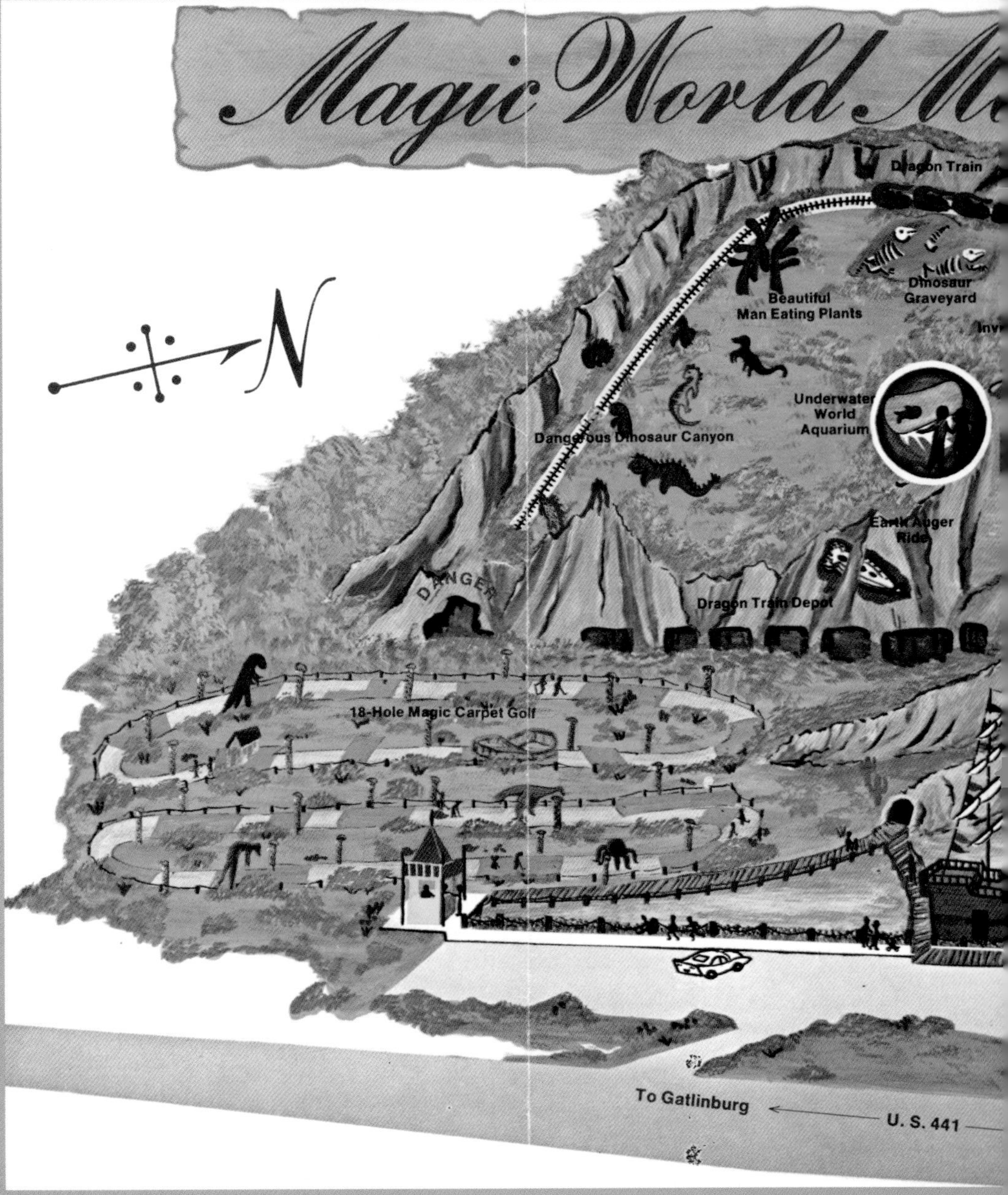

Magic World M...

Dragon Train

Beautiful
Man Eating Plants

Dinosaur
Graveyard

Inv...

Dangerous Dinosaur Canyon

Underwater
World
Aquarium

Earth Auger
Ride

DANGER

Dragon Train Depot

18-Hole Magic Carpet Golf

N

The Magnificent Journey

Lizard Cave

Unearthly Plants

Hand Fed
Fish Pool

Ghost
Grotto

Flowering Gardens

Black
Lagoon

Caveman Home

Abominable
Snowman

Magic World

Volcano Walk

Souvenir
and Gift Shop

MAGIC WORLD GIFT SHOP

Free Parking

Knoxville

A visit to Magic World included a trip on the Earth Auger, which drilled into the "center of the earth" to uncover a sinister figure inviting all to come stay with him—forever. (Cliff Holman Collection)

After surviving these hazards, visitors were confronted by the Earth Auger, which resembled an enormous drill. In veteran amusement park tradition, the would-be explorers were seated in the Earth Auger's cabin, where rotating walls seen through the windows gave the uncanny sensation of spinning around as the device bored into the "center of the earth," as the narration put it. Several spins and strobe lights later, dizzy tourists staggered from the cabin at the earth's core for sure. In case anyone needed proof, there was a sinister figure with horns and a pitchfork giving a continuous recorded spiel: "How nice of you to come visit—No one ever wants to come here—Would you like to stay a while, like maybe FOREVER? Hah hah hah hah!"

Back outside in the sunlight, the Dragon Train made regular runs through a landscape populated by the now-familiar Sidwell dinosaurs as the driver tried to be alternately educational and funny. In the final scene, the train entered a tunnel where all sorts of fearsome creatures awaited, including Sidwell's trademark giant praying mantis. Screams and groans taken from Disneyland Records' best-selling *Chilling, Thrilling Sounds of the Haunted House* album echoed through the chamber.

Magic World continued to indulge Sidwell's imaginative fantasies over the years. One of the first additions that had nothing to do with the dinosaur theme was the Flying Saucer ride. Calling it a ride was something of a misnomer, as it was actually a theater in which motion picture footage of the Smokies was projected in a 360-degree circle, surrounding the audience. The effect of soaring over the mountains in the spacecraft was compelling, even though sharp-eyed observers would occasionally notice the shadow of the helicopter carrying the cameraman.

Magic World lived up to its name with the addition of live shows featuring the prestidigitation of costumed character Merlin Rainbow. A dark ride known as the Haunted Castle proved that one did not have to have Disney's budget to achieve some effects similar to those in the Haunted Mansion. When an entire Arabian village was added in 1978 to give yet another exotic flavor, Sidwell took great pride in his "flying carpet" dark ride. As a press release described it, "It makes the rider have the feeling of soaring over ancient Arabian rooftops

Magic World's Flying Carpet dark ride sent semi-airborne visitors careening through scenes that evoked the days of the Arabian Nights.

Magic World's Confederate Critters Show was an unrepentant simplification of Disney's more famous Country Bear Jamboree. (Rod Bennett Collection)

and sandy deserts as he travels back to the days of Ali Baba and the Forty Thieves."

At the same time the Arabian city section joined Sidwell's oasis, a more indigenous cast of characters took up residence at Magic World as well. The Confederate Critters show was an animated performance that was unashamedly patterned after Disney's Country Bear Jamboree. Another press release described the down-home doins: "An electroanimated bear, who sang and played the guitar last season, now assumes the role of General Cornelius Bearpatch, and is joined by a rinky tink piano-playing hound dog called Colonel Mosby Greyhound III, and a banjo-pickin' fox that goes by the name of Major Stonewall J. Fox."

Other attractions in the neighborhood soon set out to prove that they could copy Disney's bears even more slavishly than Magic World. By 1981, two completely unrelated venues in Gatlinburg were promoting what amounted to practically the same show. Gatlinburg

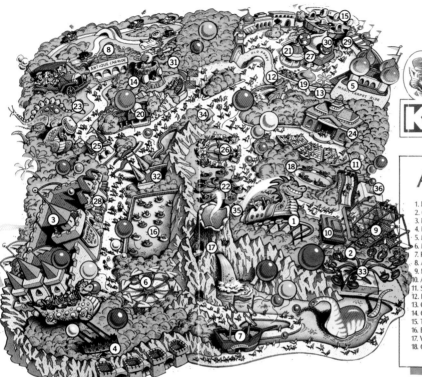

Magic World
KID'S PARK

ATTRACTIONS

1. Dragon Coaster Ride	19. Restrooms
2. Crawling Maze	20. Snackbar
3. Haunted Castle Ride	21. Ice Cream Shop
4. Flying Serpent Ride	22. Teacup Ride
5. Magic Carpet Ride	23. Dinosaur Museum
6. Mountain Glider Ride	24. Heritage Theatre
7. Pirate Ship	25. Live Fish Pond
8. Antique Car Ride	26. Pony Cart Ride
9. Net Climb	27. Arabian Gift Shop
10. Air Bounce	28. Castle Gift Shop
11. Super Slides	29. Clyde the Camel Show
12. Ball Swim	30. Fun Run Maze
13. Crawl-a-pillar	31. Family Picnic Area
14. Confederate Critter Show	32. Monster Photos
15. Tilt-a-Whirl Ride	33. Giant Spider Ride
16. Bumper Boats	34. Information Booth
17. Volcano Walk	35. Mr. Frog
18. Crank-mobile Ride	36. Punching Bags

Comparing this Magic World map from near its final season to the one shown earlier shows just how crowded the property had become.

Throughout all of its changes, this orange and yellow brontosaurus (Apatosaurus) remained in Magic World's lagoon as a roadside lure.

Place, an entertainment complex on Airport Road, advertised its Backwoods Bear Jamboree as "the zaniest bunch of animated bears, possums, gophers and crows you've ever seen, entertaining the family with the best of country music and humor." Simultaneously, Family Showstreet USA on the Parkway plugged the Smoky Mountain Bear Band: "The cutest darn show in East Tennessee, eight hilarious animated bears playing and singing foot-stompin' mountain music." Both Gatlinburg Place and Family Showstreet USA will be discussed in greater detail in chapter 6.

It was easy to tell that Magic World and its companions were trying hard to compete with the slick and fast-paced corporate theme park world. Now it was no longer enough to ride the Dragon Train and see lifeless prehistoric monsters; amusement rides and live per-

102 These three shots illustrate this site's evolution from Magic World in 1985 (top) to vacant lot in 1998 (center) to today's Professor Hacker's Lost Treasure Mini-Golf (bottom).

Other entrepreneurs sought to recapture a bit of the Sidwell magic in these attractions along U.S. 441.

formances filled every corner of the property, making it the closest thing the mountains ever had to the traditional Ferris wheel/merry-go-round style of amusement park. Ironically, the more it tried to be like other parks, the less successful it seemed to become. After the 1995 season, Magic World did a disappearing act. The original volcano tour hung on until the very end, and even three years after the park closed, broken remnants of the volcano and some of the statuary could still be seen.

No property in Pigeon Forge could be expected to remain vacant for long, and today the former Fort Weare/Magic World site is home to Professor Hacker's Lost Treasure Mini-Golf, another Sidwell family enterprise that features a concrete volcano. In a thoughtful gesture, a bronze plaque at the golf course's entrance pays tribute to the family patriarch:

The Land of Oz was justifiably proud of its museum full of props and costumes from the 1939 *Wizard of Oz* movie.

The Yellow Brick Road survives on the former Oz property today, but instead of the Emerald City, the gates at the end open onto a residential neighborhood.

The Land of Oz theme park opened atop Beech Mountain, North Carolina, in 1970. (Chris Robbins Collection)

In memory and honor of
James Q. Sidwell, Sr. (Big Jim)
March 18, 1919–April 10, 1999
For your vision, integrity, friendship and leadership

Jim Sidwell and his legacy could have been the inspiration for a new Pigeon Forge attraction that opened in October 2005, the Jurassic Jungle Boat ride. It has always been rather uncommon to find a dark ride existing as a stand-alone attraction rather than as part of a larger park, but this was one of those rare exceptions. Taking riders on a waterborne voyage through dinosaur-infested forests, the Jurassic Jungle Boats offered a combination of Sidwell's dark rides and his earlier Dragon Train, all gone high-tech.

In the next chapter, we will become better acquainted with the Robbins brothers (Grover Jr., Harry, and Spencer), whose father we met back in chapter 1, when he was inflating Blowing Rock into a major North Carolina attraction. Through some of their other enterprises, the family had become acquainted with Charlotte artist and designer Jack Pentes, and he would come to play a big part in their last and biggest tourism effort.

The Robbins clan had secured some property atop Beech Mountain, a ski resort near Banner Elk, North Carolina. They wanted to do something that would put the facilities to use during the long season when there was no snow and ice to attract skiers, and Pentes had just the idea. For years, he had wanted to build a theme park based on L. Frank Baum's immortal story *The Wizard of Oz* (and the motion picture that had been made from it). Touring the Beech Mountain site with the Robbins, Pentes was struck by the wind-deformed gnarled old trees and other exotic topography and quickly convinced the family members that their new attraction should be the Land of Oz.

It is almost foolhardy to try to discuss this park here, as its story is far too complex and intriguing to cover in a few paragraphs. It basically gave visitors the experience of living the whole Oz adventure for themselves, beginning with a simulated cyclone inside Dorothy's storm cellar. The Yellow Brick Road meandered through various scenes from the story, climaxing in a visit to the Emerald City and an audience with the Wizard (who was not a fake, as he was revealed to be in the original story and film). Guests could then board a simulated hot air balloon ride for a circuit over the green burg below.

Fortunately for the Robbins family, during the planning of their Oz park, the MGM movie studio announced a gigantic auction to clear out the decades of props and memorabilia that had accumulated over the studio's illustrious history. Spencer Robbins and an assistant attended the auction with the intention of buying everything they could afford that had been connected with the Oz film. They succeeded beyond anyone's reasonable expectations, although they did not end up owning one of the pairs of Dorothy's ruby slippers that was a high point of the auction.

According to Spencer Robbins, the Land of Oz made an agreement with MGM veteran Debbie Reynolds, who was also at the auction to secure items for her museum of old Hollywood artifacts. In exchange for her not bidding on the Oz material, Robbins promised that during the winter months, when the park was closed, the memorabilia would be loaned to her California museum. As it turned out, the expense of transporting such priceless goods was prohibitive, and once atop Beech Mountain, they never left. At least the thought counted, and Reynolds was a special guest at the park's opening on June 15, 1970, along with her later famous daughter, Carrie Fisher.

A botched robbery attempt in the last week of 1975 did not cause the loss of the movie props, but a fire that was apparently set to cover up the break-in gutted the Emerald City and otherwise made a mess out of Oz's future prospects. The Robbinses had sold the property by the time it closed at the end of the 1980 operating season, and the scenery was left to rot and be plundered by souvenir hunters. After around fifteen years of such abuse, the property was acquired by the Emerald Mountain real estate development firm, and its executives have been tireless in promoting and restoring what remains of the Land of Oz. The crowds that show up for an annual salute to the park each October certainly seem to truly believe that there's no place like Oz.

Before leaving the topic of attractions that appealed mostly to the younger set, we should briefly drop in on a now-obscure Gatlinburg entry known as the Space Ship, which sat on its launching pad awaiting the next group of paying customers. The Space Ship was basically a carnival ride in which the passengers were treated to a filmed blastoff and approach to the moon; to prove that this was not the exclusive province of the tacky and tawdry forms of tourism, a very similar ride was a part of Disneyland's futuristic Tomorrowland when that pioneering theme park opened in 1955.

There is no record of when the Gatlinburg Space Ship made its final splashdown, but we don't have much time for that right now anyway. Instead of traveling into the future, we are now going to hop on a steam locomotive and journey back-back-back into what the *Lone Ranger* announcer Fred Foy would have termed "those thrilling days of yesteryear!"

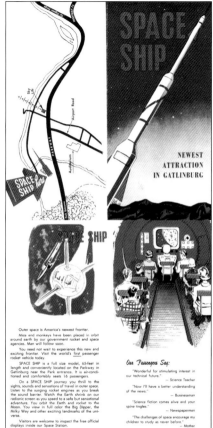

SPACE SHIP

NEWEST ATTRACTION IN GATLINBURG

Outer space is America's newest frontier.

Mice and monkeys have been placed in orbit around earth by our government rocket and space agencies. Man will follow soon.

You need not wait to experience this new and exciting frontier. Visit the world's first passenger rocket vehicle today.

SPACE SHIP is a full size model, 65-feet in length and conveniently located on the Parkway in Gatlinburg near the Park entrance. It is air-conditioned and comfortably seats 16 passengers.

On a SPACE SHIP journey you thrill to the sights, sounds and sensations of travel in outer space. Listen to the surging rocket engines as you break the sound barrier. Watch the Earth shrink on our radionic screen as you speed to a safe but sensational adventure. You orbit the Earth and rocket to the Moon. You view in full color the Big Dipper, the Milky Way and other exciting landmarks of the universe.

Visitors are welcome to inspect the free official displays inside our Space Station.

Our Passengers Say:

"Wonderful for stimulating interest in our technical future." — Science Teacher

"Now I'll have a better understanding of the news." — Businessman

"Science fiction comes alive and your spine tingles." — Newspaperman

"The challenges of space encourage my children to study as never before." — Mother

107

Gatlinburg's Space Ship attraction was a splendid example of the low-tech entertainment that could be found along the nation's tourist routes during the 1960s.

FIVE

Tweetsie and Dolly Rush for the Gold

No other aspect of the tourism industry was so tied to a current television trend as the craze for everything Western in the late 1950s and early 1960s. From the "real" West, where parks such as Knott's Berry Farm in Los Angeles and Frontier City in Oklahoma City entertained with their versions of cowboy culture, to such unlikely locales as Pennsylvania, New York, and Florida, Western parks were as much a staple of the roadside scene as motels, restaurants, service stations, and Stuckey's. The trend came early to the southern mountains, although its arrival originally had nothing to do with Marshal Dillon or Wyatt Earp.

As long ago as 1881, a railroad line had been built across the rugged mountain country between Johnson City, Tennessee, and Boone, North Carolina. The steam locomotive that plied this route became nicknamed Tweetsie because of its distinctive high-pitched whistle. Tourism was not the main purpose of the railroad, although it did serve to bring a few hardy souls into that isolated countryside. Tweetsie originally hauled iron ore and timber over its sixty-six-mile route.

As the official history reports, improvements to the highway system made such small railroads obsolete for that purpose, and Tweetsie was already on its way downhill when a 1940 flood washed away much of the track. What was left of it continued to serve until 1950,

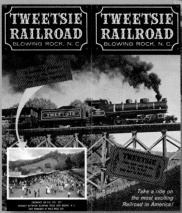

Tweetsie Railroad, near Blowing Rock, was the first and ultimately the most successful of the area's Western theme parks.

Souvenir collectors of today feel that they are on the right track if they can locate one of these rare Tweetsie Railroad coloring books. (Chris Robbins Collection)

when the railroad shut down for good. The next several years saw various interested parties fighting over Tweetsie's iron horse corpse. For a while, the engine spent time in Harrisonburg, Virginia, as the centerpiece of an attraction known as the Shenandoah Central Railroad. Then, singing cowboy Gene Autry came riding out of the sunset and offered to buy the locomotive to use in his California-based films, but even the fortunes he had amassed in the saddle were not enough to offset the costs of transporting a full-size engine from the Carolina hills to the movie capital.

Remember many pages ago, when we met Grover Robbins, the developer behind the Blowing Rock attraction? Grover's three sons, Grover Jr., Spencer, and Harry, obviously inherited their pa's knack for promotion, because in 1956, Grover Jr. bought Tweetsie's option from Gene Autry for $17,000 with the intention of moving it back to its proper neighborhood and building an attraction around it. Spencer Robbins vividly remembered the day his older brother called him to break the news about his locomotive-sized acquisition: "Our dad is going to think I've lost my mind," Grover Jr. fretted. Sane idea or not, Tweetsie's new home would be on a piece of property between Boone and Blowing Rock, and the new Tweetsie Railroad park opened on July 4, 1957.

In the beginning, the only thing to do at Tweetsie was to ride the historic train out to a picnic area and back. Since only a portion of track had been installed, the train had to travel backward to return its passengers to the entrance. Maybe that means they did not know if they were going or coming. Anyway, shortly thereafter, the track was completed around the base of Roundhouse Mountain, and Tweetsie was able to make its run without using the rearview mirror.

The trip still didn't boast much excitement, but that soon changed thanks to that glassy-eyed living room haint known as television. As I described in great detail in the book *Hi There, Boys and*

North Carolina television legend Fred Kirby became as much a part of the Tweetsie Railroad story as the locomotive itself. Here Kirby (*center*) appears with park cofounders Spencer (*left*) and Harry Robbins. (Chris Robbins collection)

FACING PAGE: Fred Kirby demonstrates how he handles people who don't watch his TV show. The folks at Tweetsie jokingly call this the "Batman photo," because all it seems to need is a giant "POW" or "BIFF" superimposed across the picture. (Chris Robbins collection)

Girls! America's Local Children's TV Programs (2001), TV stations across the country began pulling in top ratings and hefty advertising revenues with their own children's programming. These shows usually fell roughly into the categories of cowboys, sea captains, clowns, and cartoons, and WBTV in Charlotte opted for the first of those four classifications. Fred Kirby had already enjoyed a successful career as a songwriter and sometime movie cowboy when WBTV gave him his own spread, known variously as *Junior Rancho*, *The Little Rascals Club*, and *Cartoon Corral*.

In some unspecified year, but probably around 1959, WBTV used the new Tweetsie park to throw a birthday party for their resident cowpoke. To spice things up, actors from the nearby *Horn in the West* drama were recruited to suit up as renegade Indians and ornery owlhoots and attack the train during Kirby's trip with his fans. White-hatted good guy that he was, Kirby fought off the sidewinders and saved the day—and possibly saved Tweetsie too. It is uncertain just how aware Grover Robbins was of the emerging Western park craze in the rest of the country, but his railroad soon became the home of

Tweetsie Junction, complete with general store, saloon with kicking can-can girls, territorial bank, and the works.

Unlike most similar parks, one thing Tweetsie did *not* have was a periodic shootout in the street between the marshal and the bad guys. Instead, that sort of business was left to take place along the train ride itself, where Indians and robbers made every trip a perilous one. Fred Kirby returned to Tweetsie year after year, mostly during the busy summer tourist season, to serve as honorary sheriff and teach them thar varmints a thing or two about law and order, by gum.

While the railroad encircled Roundhouse Mountain, the space on top of that summit seemed to be going to waste. Breaking from the Western theme, the Robbins family installed amusement rides on top of the pinnacle, renamed it Magic Mountain, and began running a chairlift to the top. When families arrived at the peak, they found themselves in the Castle of the Sleeping Giant, a medieval fortress that was most imposing. If they wanted to impose on their host, they could climb up to the second floor and see the snoring behemoth himself. The Sleeping Giant proved to be the first collaboration between the Robbins family and Jack Pentes, whom we met in the previous chapter as the creative force behind the Land of Oz park. The Sleeping Giant display contained ample evidence of Pentes's sense of humor: he decorated the walls with such touches as an advertising calendar from "Jack & Co., Dealers in Beanstalks," with "Phone Fe-Fi-Fo-Fum."

Pentes's next project for Tweetsie outdid even his oversized sleeper, although it went in the opposite direction as far as size was concerned. In the 1970s, a miniature train was added to the Magic Mountain mix, and to give it some variety, Pentes came up with a whole storyline revolving around his "Mouse Mine No. 9." The train entered a long tunnel with walls decorated to resemble Swiss cheese,

FACING PAGE: A chairlift took visitors to Tweetsie's Castle of the Sleeping Giant, where they could have a close encounter with the snoring behemoth himself.

Jack Pentes, formerly known for his work on the Land of Oz and Castle of the Sleeping Giant, later created the Mouse Mine Ride for Tweetsie Railroad.

and there before riders' eyes was a fluorescent tableau of cartoony rodents engaged in every sort of mining activity. The display was a terrific example of Pentes's talents as a store window designer and continues to delight today's children, even though they're supposed to be too sophisticated for such simple sights. The Sleeping Giant, for his part, did not survive—but not because of Jack or other giant killers. Being made of papier-mâché, the old snorer was just not built to survive in such an inhospitable environment. His former castle is now an open-air station for the skylift, and no one seems to miss his somnambulant presence.

Meanwhile, back down in Tweetsie Junction, things went along pretty much as they always had. That is, until the dark days of the 1970s, when tourism as a whole took a hit it had not experienced since World War II. Rising fuel costs had already done their part to siphon the flow of tourists who were out for joy rides, and when gas rationing caused service stations to close on Sundays, everyone in the tourist business felt it. As Spencer Robbins said, "In the beginning, if we had two thousand people on Saturday, we knew we'd have four thousand people on Sunday. Well, after the closing of the service stations, that trend reversed. If we had two thousand people on Saturday we'd have only one thousand on Sunday—and it has never gone back. To this day, Sunday is always just half of what Saturday was."

More troubles reared their ugly heads after the dawn of the twenty-first century. When the Robbins family first acquired the property for their attraction, they did so under a fifty-year lease. This would seem to be plenty, since as they explain, in 1957 the assumption was that in fifty years people would be flying about in spaceships and no one would care about an antique train. However, as the end of the lease approached in 2007, the family was caught in the predicament of having a legend in southern tourism sitting on land that had greatly increased in value. Several landowners were licking their chops at the prospect of selling that parcel for a shopping center or housing development, putting the railroad out to pasture. The saga has not yet been resolved. The venerable locomotive may yet have to change its trademark whistle to play "Tweet, Tweet, Tweetsie Goodbye."

While Tweetsie was tootling around near Blowing Rock, another Western park was materializing down at Maggie Valley, not far from Cherokee. The responsible party was R. B. Coburn, a former Holiday Inn innkeeper from Orangeburg, South Carolina. In 1960, Coburn bought some mountaintop property at Maggie Valley with the intention of putting in a chairlift—possibly inspired by the Gatlinburg Sky Lift ride. After he purchased the property but before construction began, Coburn had an epiphany that would change his plans.

The Coburn family went on a trip to the West Coast, visiting those two theme park titans, Disneyland and Knott's Berry Farm. On the way out, they stopped in Oklahoma City and stayed at the Holiday Inn (since Coburn was loyal to the Great Sign that fed him) next door to the Frontier City theme park. As a lifelong Western movie devotee, Coburn was enchanted by Frontier City, and when he got to California and saw what Knott's had done with the concept and

Close examination of this early Ghost Town in the Sky souvenir booklet shows that artwork for the buildings and chairlift were superimposed onto a photograph of the mountain.

Like any other Western theme park, Ghost Town in the Sky featured periodic shootouts between the marshal and the no-good snakes in the weeds who tried to disturb the peace. On the balcony above, park owner R. B. Coburn is designated as the town mayor.

R. B. Coburn opened his own Western park atop a mountain at Maggie Valley, North Carolina, in 1961. This is one of the few advertising items to refer to it as Ghost Mountain Park.

how Disneyland had made a destination out of its Frontierland section, he knew what he was going to do back home. "I'm going to put a Western town on top of that mountain," he declared, and that is how Ghost Town in the Sky came into being.

Coburn enlisted the expertise of former movie set designer Russell Pearson, who had been responsible for Frontier City as well as Silver Dollar City in Missouri and who had the reputation of being an old Western character himself. Pearson and Coburn would work together on future attractions, with Pearson always striving mightily to ensure that each was historically accurate. This occasionally worked against the best interests of tourism and promotion, so compromises were sometimes necessary.

Speaking of not-so-authentic concepts folded into the Western theme, Ghost Town still had room for Coburn's original chairlift idea. In fact, when the park opened in June 1961, that was the main way of transporting guests from the parking area to the town. An incline railway and bus service were provided for those who preferred solid ground beneath their feet. Once at the top, the traditional Western saga played itself out, with regularly scheduled bank robberies foiled by the timely arrival of the town marshal. Drawing on television's popularity, the skits sometimes involved such famed Western characters as Doc Holliday and Bat Masterson.

Whenever shootists were not shooting it out on the streets, tourists had plenty of other things with which to occupy themselves. The Red Dog Saloon featured the ever-popular dancing girls, while the blacksmith shop, Indian village trading post, and community church gave glimpses into other aspects of frontier life. (The church was the genuine article, with various local congregations taking turns holding services there on Sunday afternoons.) The Ghost Mine Rock Shop offered various minerals and stones for sale and served as a front for a funhouse-type walk-through in which "spooks walk along the pathway with you as you wander by," according to the press materials.

Coburn knew when he had a good thing, and the year after opening Ghost Town in the Sky, he announced plans for his even larger Western town, Six Gun Territory, near Silver Springs, Florida. After that one was off and galloping, he returned to the North Carolina hills for one more project, and we will catch up with him on that one shortly.

Meanwhile, were Grover, Spencer and Harry Robbins just twiddling their thumbs at Tweetsie? You bet your boiler they weren't. The same year that Coburn opened Ghost Town in the Sky, the Robbins brothers sought to duplicate their Tweetsie complex over the mountains in Pigeon Forge, and that attraction would come to have far-reaching effects on the area's tourism history.

While a train ride would still be the centerpiece of their new park, the Robbinses chose not simply to duplicate the milieu of Tweetsie. Instead, taking their cue from the contemporary Civil War centennial observance, they came up with a concept that might be considered— shall we say—rather politically incorrect today. Clamber aboard the Rebel Railroad, as the Pigeon Forge park was called, and listen to part of its publicity: "This unusual railroad operates over a scenic route to Fort Agony, affording the passengers unmatched views of the beautiful Smoky Mountains, plus the excitement of running the Yankee

The Robbins brothers of Tweetsie Railroad fame sought to duplicate their success by opening the Rebel Railroad in Pigeon Forge in 1961.

The Rebel Railroad initially took the traditional cowboys and Indians and outlaws theme and converted it into Rebels versus Yankees. This being Tennessee, the bluecoats always lost.

blockade. Along the way, the Rebel chugs up steep grades, pounds around curves, through cuts and over fills, to bring supplies to Fort Agony under Yankee fire. Finally the Rebel returns in triumphant glory to Rebeltown, safe behind Confederate lines."

Yes suh, you could bet a purty that those who visited the Rebel Railroad were expected to thoroughly sympathize with the Confederate cause. Possibly no other attraction took the standard Indians/train robbers shtick and translated it into Yankee/Confederate terminology. Those who visited the Rebel Railroad during this period remember the skits in which the bluecoats would attack the train only to be routed by the boys in gray. Comedy frequently would ensue, such as one of the fleeing Yankees having the seat of his pants shot out, revealing red long johns underneath.

Other than these new spins on American history, the rest of the Rebel Railroad complex looked much like that at Tweetsie. Rebeltown was equivalent to Tweetsie Junction, with the saloon, blacksmith shop, general store, and other frontier trappings. This would come to serve the attraction well, because once the enthusiasm for the Civil War began wearing off, the attraction underwent a chameleon-like change and took on a completely new identity.

In 1964, minor cosmetic surgery transformed the Rebel Railroad into Goldrush Junction, evoking the days of prospectors and claim jumpers rather than magnolias and mint juleps. The train and the frontier-style town remained the same, except for the disappearance of the Confederate flags. The Yankees who periodically attacked the train also went back north, replaced by those old standbys, marauding Indians and slimy gold thieves.

The park began to show a hitherto unevidenced interest in amusement rides to go along with the traditional railroad. One of its first acquisitions was the log flume ride that had operated at the 1964–65 New York World's Fair. When that fair reached the end of

Compare this brochure with the one for Tweetsie Railroad shown earlier in this chapter. The locomotive shown here is Tweetsie rather than the one at Pigeon Forge.

With the Civil War centennial winding down, the Rebel Railroad was converted into Goldrush Junction in 1964. At far left is the log flume ride that was transplanted from the New York World's Fair.

its run, Goldrush Junction purchased half of the flume ride, while the other half went even further south and ended up at the Pirate's World amusement park at Dania, Florida. The flume ride was a great fit for Goldrush's new wild and woolly theme.

All of these changes must have worked well, because as Goldrush Junction the park was a bigger gold mine than it had ever been as the Rebel Railroad. Its biggest days lay ahead, but before getting into that part of the story, we now have to return to North Carolina to see what Coburn had been up to since producing his Ghost Town in the Sky out of the ether.

When we last left them, you will recall, Coburn and his park designer pardner, Russell Pearson, had moseyed on down to Florida to open Six Gun Territory, but by 1965 they were a-hankerin' to do something else in the Great Smokies, where they could feature pine trees instead of palm trees. They set their sights on Cherokee, where a Western park would fit right in with the Plains Indians–inspired costumes and accoutrements that were so prevalent.

The tourism industry is full of unsolved mysteries, as we have already seen in this book and others on the subject, and right here is where we find another of those. While Coburn and Pearson were fiddling around in Florida, a park calling itself Cherokee Wonderland

Cherokee Wonderland was a small theme park that evolved into R. B. Coburn's third big Western attraction, Frontier Land.

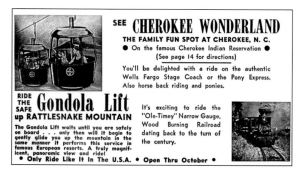

had opened on the reservation in the hills. Cherokee Wonderland advertised itself as "the fabulous fun spot in the Smokies," touting its primary points of interest: "Designed for the entire family, you may ride the gondola family lift up the mountain, or ride the 'ole-timey' narrow gauge railroad around Oconaluftee River. Also take a different ride in the historic Wells Fargo Stage Coach."

The mysterious question is whether Coburn bought Cherokee Wonderland and turned it into his own attraction or whether he started from scratch, perhaps moving some of the older park's elements to a new location. In any case, in 1965 Coburn opened Frontier Land in Cherokee, and the Wonderland apparently disappeared down a rabbit hole. (It may be no small coincidence that Coburn gave his latest park the same name as one of the sections of Disneyland that had inspired him to go into the amusement business in the first place, although he chose to spell it as two words rather than Disney's one.)

Much about Frontier Land was quite familiar, since by that time Coburn and Pearson (who died just before the new park's opening) were a couple of old cowhands at that game. Because of its location, Frontier Land played up the soldiers-Indians conflict a little more prominently than either Ghost Town in the Sky or Six Gun Territory. To make sure that tourists could tell the good guys from the bad, Frontier Land issued promotional flyers picturing all the major players on each side, including fighting Indians Chief Running Horse, Yellow Feathers, and the Cherokee Kid. (What, no cowardly Chief Yellow Streak?) The rest of the hardy pioneers were based out of Fort Cherokee, where the cavalry looked like something straight out of *F Troop*. Going along with the format established at his other parks, Coburn supplemented the frontier frolics with amusement rides of a more modern flavor.

Similar changes were taking place back at Goldrush Junction.

This spectacular aerial shot of Frontier Land shows not only the entire complex—which was located where Cherokee's Harrah's Casino now sits—but also interesting artifacts along the periphery as well. Eagle-eyed readers will be able to spot the Putt-Putt Golf course, a pointy-roofed restaurant with a Kentucky Fried Chicken bucket in front, and the distinctive shape of the Cyclorama of the Cherokee Indian building.

FRONTIER LAND . . .

FORT CHEROKEE

INDIAN TERRITORY U.S.A.

PIONEER JUNCTION

GLAMOUR

ADVENTURE

ACTION

EXPLODING WITH EXCITEMENT

Frontier Land's advertising played up most of the same features that could be found in Coburn's other parks but with special emphasis on the confrontations between the Indians and the cavalry.

Following the death of Grover Robbins Jr. in 1970, the family sold the park to—get this—the Cleveland Browns football team. Just why the Browns thought they could make a touchdown with an amusement park in Pigeon Forge is enough to make anyone fumble for an answer, but the team carried the ball for a few years.

In April 1976, the Browns' interest was bought out by Jack and Pete Herschend, the brothers who had made such a destination out of Silver Dollar City in southern Missouri. Longtime Herschend employee Ted Miller explained just how and why the Ozark tycoons became interested in Goldrush Junction: "In the 1970s, you'll remember, we had the energy crisis, and because Silver Dollar City was so far from any metro markets, we made the decision that we needed to diversify our assets, and develop another Silver Dollar City in an area that was close to a high density population. That way, if there was another energy crisis, maybe the new park would fare okay even if the other one suffered."

Contrary to what one might suspect, the Herschends did not necessarily look to purchase an existing park. They scouted locations in Indiana and Kentucky for possible property on which to build a new Silver Dollar City. When they turned to the tourism-happy world of the Great Smokies, one piece of property they considered was an apple orchard on Highway 321 outside Gatlinburg. "We could see that one wasn't going to work," said Miller, "because the city of Gatlinburg wouldn't let us put a directional sign to show the way. The Highway 321 intersection is right in the middle of town, and they didn't want us directing traffic out of Gatlinburg! Then, also, we found out that Goldrush Junction was for sale anyway, and we got concerned that a potential major theme park buyer might come along and we'd have a competitor right there on the inbound route. So, we finally decided that purchasing Goldrush was probably our best option."

For the 1976 season, the park operated under the name of the

New Goldrush, but by the next year it had been brought into the Silver Dollar City mold of crafts and mountain heritage, which more than fit the Smokies' established image. Trying to keep the park as faithful as possible, Silver Dollar City at first removed the amusement rides and sold them off to other parks; soon thereafter, the Herschends found that they had just alienated a large portion of their potential audience, and so a completely new area for rides was added in 1980. One of these was a dark ride of the Disney or Six Flags type, the Flooded Mine. Passengers rode in boats through scenes of somewhat desperate convicts trying to escape from their underground work detail, a ride that was faintly reminiscent of Disney's Pirates of the Caribbean. Despite its novelty, the Flooded Mine just did not strike the right chords with people who were at Silver Dollar City for a day's fun. According to Miller, no matter how much was done or changed to lighten up the ride and make it funnier, there was just something inherently uncomfortable about seeing people—prisoners or no—trapped in a flooding mine shaft and facing certain death. It didn't do a thing to make anyone's day more enjoyable, so it was eventually released from its shackles. (For whatever reason, the Flooded Mine ride at the original Silver Dollar City in Missouri continues to thrive.)

The rest of the Pigeon Forge attraction was more successful than the dark ride idea, and by the mid-1980s it had drawn the attention of one of country music's brightest bulbs, Dolly Parton. The fact that Parton had been born within a few miles of Pigeon Forge and still had cousins by the dozens in the area no doubt gave her a special interest in the region. According to Miller, in the early 1980s it became a tradition for Parton to treat her young nieces and nephews to a day at Silver Dollar City, and during one such visit she remarked about how much fun it would be to have a theme park of her own.

Then, Miller says, one day Parton appeared on a Barbara Walters

FAR LEFT: To no one's surprise, Silver Dollar City chose to emphasize its proven winning blend of folk art and down-home entertainment rather than cowboys and shoot-'em-ups.

LEFT: The Flooded Mine dark ride at Silver Dollar City was supposed to be humorous, in the vein of Disney's Pirates of the Caribbean, but the park found that there was really no way to make scenes of doomed convicts seem like fun.

BELOW: By the 1980s, Silver Dollar City had grown so much that it was totally unrecognizable as the one-time Rebel Railroad.

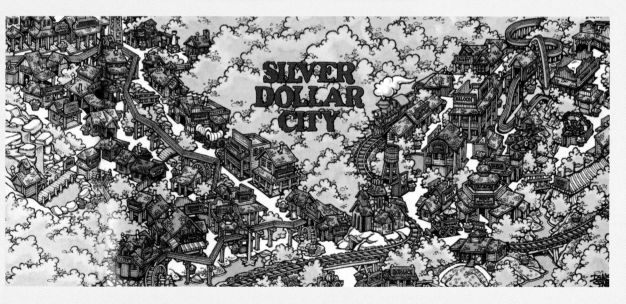

television show and announced that she was going to build a park called Dollywood somewhere in the Smoky Mountains area. This sent the folks at Silver Dollar City into a hissy fit, because just as they had purchased Goldrush Junction to keep a competitor from getting it, now they were faced with the prospect of an even bigger competitor with unlimited resources and name recognition. Deciding "If ya can't beat 'em, at least jine up with 'em," they prepared a proposal that would make Parton a part owner of Silver Dollar City and change its name.

Regardless of her carefully crafted public image—one of her favorite and most quoted lines was, "It takes a lot of money to look this cheap"—Parton obviously did not obtain Nashville superstar status by being a boob. Shrewd businessperson that she was, Parton took up the Herschend brothers on their offer, and in May 1986 Silver Dollar City opened under the Dollywood name.

Nothing has to be explained here about what a tourist magnet Dollywood turned out to be. Pigeon Forge was already experiencing a growth spurt when the name change occurred, and the years that followed would transform the formerly tiny town into a tourist strip of major proportions. Through it all, the basic structures of Dollywood are much the same ones that began during its Rebel Railroad days, although so much remodeling has been done that they are frequently unrecognizable. The World's Fair log flume has long since been demolished, and the Western shoot-'em-up theme fired its last bullet years ago, but who can tell what might have been Pigeon Forge's fate today had it not been for that long-ago tourism craze for cowboys and Indians?

While all of these major players were whooping it up, other mavericks just ambled in, sat a spell, and then continued on their way into oblivion. Some of them did not even bother with the Western town setting, relying totally on their train rides. The Bear Creek Junction Railroad made its first run in June 1966, offering trips through Nantahala Gorge between Topton and Robbinsville, North Carolina. The ride fronted a museum of railroad memorabilia, including vintage sleeping, eating, and freight cars. Since there wasn't an abundance of room to run a train around Ghost Town in the Sky, a nearby attraction was known as the Maggie Valley Railroad, in partnership with the Gunfighters Museum. The former half of the attraction took riders five miles back into the hills aboard a vintage iron horse, while the museum displayed "the rarest and largest collection of authenticated outlaw and frontier guns, photographs, mementoes and material ever assembled."

Strictly for the younger set, two miniature trains vied to give the same kind of experience. Smoky Poky in Pigeon Forge and Old Smoky in Cherokee looked and sounded enough alike to be blood brothers; it is very possible that they were the same attraction, moved from one locale to the other, since no evidence indicates that they operated during the same period. The Cherokee/Old Smoky version advertised itself as "a one-mile trip, two rounds, through the 'great swamp.'" (If they had called the great swamp the Okefenokee, they would have had the makings of yet another dark ride, but Six Flags Over Georgia beat them to it.)

Probably the most ambitious of the "forgotten" Western parks was Gold Mountain, near Franklin, North Carolina, which opened in 1967. Inasmuch as it was located on top of a mountain and accessed by chairlift, tourists could have been forgiven for getting it confused with Ghost Town in the Sky. Gold Mountain was based on the historical fact that Hernando de Soto had indeed discovered gold in the area and on the legend that an untapped gold mine remained nearby. One of its attractions was a walk-through tour of the supposed former mine shafts inside the mountain, complete with animated miners. While no one ever found enough gold in the shafts to make

Scrooge McDuck go nuts, the tunnels were loaded with pyrite, better known as fool's gold, and under the right lighting, the effect was satisfactory. Strategically timed explosions would erupt from the mine to remind people that it was there.

In 1969, Charles Tombras, operator of the Lost Sea at Sweetwater, Tennessee, bought the Gold Mountain attraction, now known as Gold City. Tombras said adios to its de Soto/Spanish theme, converting it to the standard Western park elements. To bring it in line with his other attraction, in 1970 the name was again changed, to the Lost Mine. Tombras enlisted family friend Archie Campbell of *Grand Ole Opry* and *Hee Haw* fame to act as the park's official spokesperson, but even the combined influence of Campbell's Pee Little Thrigs and Rindercellar was not enough to compensate for the Lost Mine's somewhat isolated status, removed from the rest of the area's burgeoning tourist centers. A 1972 fire closed the Lost Mine for a season, after which it was purchased by Florida businessman Leo Furlong. The new owner rebuilt that which had burned and tried to make a go of it one more time, but by 1975 the end had come. According to former park manager Andy Smalls, in recent years the chairlift has begun hauling visitors to the top once more, where they are allowed to wander through the uninhabited town ruins. The Lost Mine itself, with its abundance of pyrite and animated figures, is no longer accessible, but it is intriguing to speculate that the dioramas may still be entombed in those sealed-off shafts.

(For his part, Campbell may well have used his experience with Gold City/Lost Mine and its successes and failures to learn valuable lessons. As chapter 6 will show, he became a tourism tycoon on his own in Pigeon Forge and Gatlinburg.)

By the 1980s, even the big guns in the Western park race had to face the fact that their genre was no longer as popular as it had once been. Coburn sold his two North Carolina parks and the one

Near Franklin, North Carolina, this attraction known successively as Gold Mountain, Gold City, and the Lost Mine tried valiantly to overcome its remote location.

Ride the Incline Railway to .....
GHOST TOWN
MAGGIE VALLEY, N.C.
U.S. 19

R. B. Coburn eventually regained control of Ghost Town in the Sky and continued operating it until the end of the 2002 season. Its closing dealt a major blow to Maggie Valley's once-thriving tourist industry.

in Florida to National Services Industries, which soon used its vast corporate wisdom to drive all three of them into the ground. Six Gun Territory closed in 1984, but Ghost Town in the Sky doggedly stuck in the saddle. In the late 1980s, Coburn bought back Ghost Town for sentimental purposes and continued to operate it much as he always had until it succumbed to the changing market in 2002. (When Ghost Town became a ghost for real, it took much of Maggie Valley's tourism infrastructure with it, leaving scores of empty former restaurants, motels, and souvenir shops in its wake.)

As for what was once Coburn's third park, Frontier Land bit the dust in 1983, just before Six Gun Territory. Unlike Ghost Town in Maggie Valley, Frontier Land's presence was hardly missed in Cherokee. The property was used for a water park for a while but today is home to the mammoth Harrah's Casino, and the gambling industry seems to have rendered the rest of the town's more hokey attractions obsolete. Nothing visible remains of Frontier Land, and memories tend to get short when money—in the volumes taken in by the casino, at least—is involved.

And so, as our heroes ride off into the sunset with their eyeshades on and one hand operating the roulette wheel, we bid a fond farewell to the ersatz towns of the Old West that once found homes in the Southeast. Were they real, or were they all just hallucinations of some old cowpoke who had been on the trail too long?

The American Historical Wax Museum moved into Gatlinburg's former town movie theater building in the early 1960s.

Gatlinburg's
AMERICAN HISTORICAL
WAX MUSEUM

OPEN DAILY - ALL YEAR - Including Sunday
ON THE PARKWAY
GATLINBURG, TENNESSEE

137

$$\text{SIX}$$

Here Come the Celebrities, Believe It or Not

For those who like to appoint themselves as critics, I will admit up front that the two topics in this chapter might seem like something of a stretch to combine together. Keep reading, and you will see just how clever I really was in doing so. (And besides, there was no other way of getting both of them covered in this book. So there.)

For a while in the 1990s, it appeared that the entire strip of U.S. 441 from Sevierville to Gatlinburg in Tennessee was poised to become the next Branson, Missouri. Celebrity theaters and big-name stars popped up as if someone had been planting them as seeds. We'll talk about that in a few pages, but the fact is that the first celebrities to arrive in the area did not sing, dance, or tell jokes. In fact, they could not even move.

The American Historical Wax Museum moved into Gatlinburg's former movie theater building sometime between 1963 and 1966. The fact that it was a product of interests far from the mountain town itself has made it most difficult to pinpoint any specifics about the date or circumstances of its origin. What is known is that Gatlinburg's wax museum shared a common ownership with similar displays in Gettysburg, Pennsylvania, and Williamsburg, Virginia. Most likely Gatlinburg was chosen as the site for this venture because of the success of Christus Gardens, the only previous attempt to pour wax figures into the area's mold of tourist attractions.

The owners of the American Historical Wax Museum later opened another exhibit, Stars over Gatlinburg, that featured re-creations of famous movie scenes and personalities.

Some wax museums defined history a bit loosely, indiscriminately mixing patriotic scenes with religious scenes and those re-creating the celebrity world of Hollywood. (The chain of Tussaud wax museums was among those that followed this pattern.) However, like Christus Gardens, the American Historical Wax Museum found a theme and stubbornly stuck to it. As the name implied, American history was the textbook from which it took its rules, whether involving the patriots of colonial days, cultural leaders such as Sequoyah, or heroes of the twentieth century, such as Sergeant Alvin York. The museum also adapted to changing times, adding dioramas depicting the shooting of Lee Harvey Oswald and the moon walk of Neil Armstrong as evolving history dictated.

Speaking of evolving, the original museum's limitation to history at a national level later forced its owners to open a second location, Stars over Gatlinburg, that could encompass all the Hollywood and music stars excluded from the original. Many of these faux celebrities did not closely resemble the famous faces on which they were supposed to be based. Both wax museums eventually suffered a meltdown, and their collections were pulled from Gatlinburg and moved elsewhere. Their subsequent fate is unknown, but they likely still inhabit some tourist center and pull in visitors who want to rub wax elbows with history's finest.

In 2004, screen legend Debbie Reynolds announced that Pigeon Forge would become the new home for her Hollywood Motion Picture Museum, an unparalleled collection of props and other memorabilia from the golden age of the movies. Now, just think—come on, I know you can do it—this is the selfsame museum that was intended to have joint custody of the movie props on exhibit at the Land of Oz park way back in 1970. Its Pigeon Forge opening was scheduled for June 2006. By the time you read this, presumably the former props and costumes used by John Wayne, Barbra Streisand, Laurel and Hardy, and their famous friends will be packing 'em in once again.

Celebrities of a different type hung around in a Gatlinburg institution—and some of them deserved to be institutionalized—that made its debut in 1969. Ripley's Believe It or Not! Museum had already established successful locations in Florida, New York, and California before the Gatlinburg location opened, but once the Ripley brand of sensationalism invaded the mountains, it threatened almost to take over the entire town.

Debbie Reynolds was supposed to have borrowed the movie costumes and props from the Land of Oz theme park during the off-season for her Hollywood history museum. In 2004, she announced plans to move her collection to Pigeon Forge.

Although Ripley's stars were of a somewhat different caliber than the George Washingtons and Bob Hopes who hung out at the other museums, they all became familiar sights to those who visited the exhibit over the years. Who could forget the "man with a hole in his head" who walked around with a lighted candle stuck in the top of his skull; the "double eyed man," who had four pupils, the better to see you with, my dear; the boy who died of old age when he was seven years old (most kids of that age have a similar effect on their parents); the "man who died laughing," accompanied by a continuous recorded loop of hysterical ha-has; and other oddities of nature, animal, vegetable, and mineral.

HISTORY RECREATED IN CANDY

Only at Ripley's Believe It Or Not! Museum could you ever hope to see a scale model as spectacular as the *CIRCUS MAXIMUS*, the great Roman amphitheatre where thousands of Christians met their death in the days of Emperor Nero. The replica was created with *unbelievable* artistry by Laszlo Dorogi, famed Las Vegas Pastry Chef — out of 100 lbs. of Icing Sugar!

LINCOLN'S LOG CABIN

This unusual replica of our great P
awarded a special citation for the mo
can Numismatic Convention of 196
and in case you're in no mood for c
tains 9,600 uncirculated Lincoln penr

THERE REALLY WAS A MOTHER GOOSE

Children have always known it . . . now here is proof for adults too. Her maiden name was Elizabeth Foster and she married Isaac Goose in 1692. When you learn how many children she had you'll know why she wrote nursery rhymes.

CANNIBAL CURIO

There are only three examples of this rare oddity in America, and Ripley's have two of them. If you are one of those people who believe only what they can see, take the opportunity to visit Gatlinburg's Believe It Or Not! Museum and see this *Human Ceremonial Skull* from Dutch New Guinea.

SHIP OF BONES

What most people discard, Chef Johann Zellweger transforms into ships like the Santa Maria, pictured here. Osseous (Bony) Sculpture would be an accurate description of such artworks, since they are made up entirely of chicken and turkey bones!

These were only a few of the strange sights lurking in Gatlinburg's original version of Ripley's Believe It or Not! Museum, all of which were destroyed by fire in 1992.

WALK THRU THE WORLD'S STRANGEST GRAVEYARD

Robert Ripley was the first Journalist of importance to catalog and publish the curious epitaphs that some people have mounted over the graves of their "Dearly Departed". At the Ripley Museum you can read for yourself the best of these fascinating and humorous epitaphs found in sobriety of graveyards throughout the world.

...mble birthplace was ...e exhibit at the Ameri-...veighs over 175 lbs, ...n tell you . . . it con-

...-HEADED CALF

...d in whole or part, such ...e creatures were once ...as something of super-...igin and were referred ...onsters". No less an ...than Dr. C. H. Forth-...Oklahoma, witnessed ...f this exhibit.

THE WORLD'S SMALLEST VIOLIN

Beautifully toned, only 5½" long. Though size limits volume, this hand crafted replica was actually played by its maker on Ripley's radio show.

THE MAN OF CHAINS

This curious fellow also known as the "Jingling Fakir" is just one of many characters reproduced life-size from Ripley's world famous pocket books. He is shown complete with his groaning load of 670 lbs. which he dragged through the streets of Lahore, India.

These photos illustrate the evolution of the Ripley's building from the original rather nondescript one (*top*) to a more creative facade (*center*) to the three-story monolith that was rebuilt after the disastrous 1992 fire.

Don't Miss.......
Gatlinburg's Newest
- - - - - ATTRACTION - - - - -
MUSEUM OF WITCHCRAFT & MAGIC

IT'S FOR ALL THE FAMILY!

IT'S ALL FOR FUN!

FREE MAGIC SHOWS BY "CONLEY" (RENOWNED MAGICIAN)

Are you a witch?   Did you marry one?
Have you seen a crystal ball that talks?

The Ripley Artists Have Taken 3 Years In Planning — And Now Present To You, This Adventure Of Man And His Superstitions.

Ripley's first branched out of its own museum when it opened the Museum of Witchcraft and Magic in 1972.

When the original Gatlinburg Ripley's building burned to the ground in 1992, some people might have wondered whether the fire was real or just a publicity stunt. It was real enough, though, and spelled the end for most of those well-established displays. Tourism historian Rod Bennett said that one exhibit in particular seemed to embody what the museum was all about: "In my mind's eye I see the laughing Frenchman, giggling while Rome burns, face streaming with tears, and being slowly reduced to a sizzling puddle of beeswax on the floor. In my fancy, his eternal laugh track was the last thing to go. In my imagination I hear that hidden tape player sputtering to a stop only as the last smoldering stick of Ripley's museum falls into a gigantic heap of charcoal and ash."

Of course, Ripley's had not made its believe-it-or-not reputation by doing the expected, and being destroyed by fire did not end its Gatlinburg career. After three years of rebuilding, the museum opened in a new three-story structure that closely resembled the crumbling victim of an earthquake. While most of the old displays did not rise from the ashes, a whole new plethora of kooky sights rushed in to fill the gap, and for the first time the museum heavily involved hands-on exhibits, in the fashion of the newer breed of children's science museums. Yes, Ripley's had indeed come to Gatlinburg to stay.

This was especially true for those who were paying close attention to the projects of the Ripley organization that were not directly related to the Believe It or Not! Museum. One of the earliest Ripley spin-offs in Gatlinburg opened in 1972 as the Museum of Witchcraft and Magic. Dedicated to artifacts of the occult, this museum seemed somewhat misplaced in the same Bible Belt where dwelt Christus Gardens. Perhaps for this reason, by 1975 the name had been altered to Dr. Gardner's Museum of Magic and Superstition, but it remained under Ripley ownership.

The World's Largest Exhibition of Grand Illusions gathered from Around the World!

BEAUTY AND THE BEAST
Recreated as never before.

OUT OF THIS WORLD!!!
Action with the spectacular RD2 in a scene inspired by Star Wars.

FANTASY
Becomes reality when you talk to Ali Baba's Genie trapped inside a glass bottle forever. Over 7 million people have!

MAGICAL
Illusions so grand that the creators have sworn to reveal the secrets only after death.

LAUGH
Along with some of the all time comedy greats as they treat you to some of the greatest illusions ever created.

ESCA
into the p when the amazing Houdini recreates famous Chinese Torture Escape.

By the beginning of the twenty-first century, Ripley properties occupied more of Gatlinburg than any other single entity's holdings. In Ripley's Moving Theater, the seats traveled along with whatever action was happening on the screen; Ripley's Aquarium of the Smokies was part of a renewed craze for aquatic exhibits that swept the South during the 1990s; and Ripley's Davy Crockett Mini-Golf showed that the company's ingenuity could be put to use in the same territory pioneered by Jolly Golf (on whose former property the course was built).

The Ripley company ventured into the genre of haunted house attractions with Ripley's Haunted Adventure, naturally taking the concept in directions unforeseen by those tourism pioneers who once made their living by designing such walk-through environments. One of those old-timers was Vincent "Val" Valentine, whose career as an artist dated back to the Max Fleischer animation studio in Miami. As has been well documented in other books, Valentine became involved in Florida tourism in the area around Silver Springs in the 1950s and by 1965 had shifted his base of operations to Panama City Beach. Valentine was responsible for many of the attractions along that goofy strip of U.S. 98, including the famed Old House at the Miracle Strip Amusement Park.

Valentine had gone on to design haunted houses for other tourist centers, including the Wisconsin Dells, and in 1981 he brought his own form of creepiness to Gatlinburg with his Mysterious Mansion. At the time, Valentine was quoted as saying, "I have always had the conviction that the haunted house concept had a universal appeal, and that people in general love to be scared—especially if they scared themselves." This statement was the key to Valentine's preferred format for his heebie-jeebie-producing attractions: rather than relying on costumed performers and mechanical monsters, Valentine devised ways to have the visitors thoroughly creep themselves out from

FACING PAGE: The World of Illusions museum was one of many attractions that came to the Smokies in Ripley's wake. Any museum that featured *Star Wars* characters keeping company with Frankenstein's monster and Groucho Marx had to be trying to prove something to the Believe It or Not! crowd.

145

a psychological standpoint. One of his favorite tricks was to have a balcony overlooking a grand entrance hallway. When an unsuspecting person stepped out onto the balcony for a better look, the whole thing would suddenly tilt forward as if to collapse and drop the victim several stories below.

Valentine was also concerned that his creations not become too macabre. He countered the chills with snickers, as with his wishing well. "The sign said to drop in a quarter, and if the skeleton appeared at the bottom, your wish MIGHT come true," he explained, leaving the necessary loophole. Naturally, the skeleton appeared for everyone, responding to coin tosses with sarcastic lines such as, "Ah, the last of the big-time spenders."

As we have seen time and time again in this book, nothing proves success as well as imitation, so Ripley's too inspired some near-clones in its immediate neighborhood. Most notable of these was the Guinness Hall of World Records, which brought its record-setters to

Florida tourism veteran Val Valentine, of Silver Springs and Miracle Strip Amusement Park fame, built Gatlinburg's Mysterious Mansion in 1981. (Val Valentine Collection)

life in much the same form Ripley's used. A museum with the almost unpronounceable name Sciential opened in 1968 as "an authentic tour of modern science." Get a load of the up-to-date cutting edge technology it exhibited: "Through usage of sight, sound, action and viewer participation, a unique series of exhibits will involve visitors in a variety of experiences, ranging from seeing themselves on television to operating an abacus to playing computerized tic-tac-toe." Boy howdy, that'll sure pull the young 'uns away from their Nintendos today.

Those who were kooky for the spooky had even more choices. One Gatlinburg attraction that first showed its ectoplasm in the 1980s and continues its tradition today didn't mince words, simply calling itself Hauntings. What was it? Obviously the whole idea was to pay the admission fee and find out. No help was forthcoming from its description, which read, "Real live ghost shows [an oxymoron if there ever was one] every 20 minutes that explore the unknown. Eerie figures from the world beyond, strange lights and sounds, bizarre manifestations, objects moving mysteriously, and screams from a participating audience seven days a week." You'd think the audience would be tired of screaming for that long, wouldn't you?

Of course, seeing peculiar sights—of the supernatural or subnatural type—had been a tourism fixture since Robert Ripley was still alive at those roadside museums of optical illusions that usually billed themselves as "mystery houses." While they thrived nationwide, a thick concentration of them occurred in the mountains—possibly because the terrain seemed so exotic to nonresidents in the first place. One Mystery Hill, near Blowing Rock, dated to 1948 and explained how its odd occurrences originated: "It seemed the gravitational pull on the side of the mountain caused unusual things to happen," it gravely stated. The Mystery House at Cherokee made similar claims: "Feel the terrifyingly powerful pull of the earth in this house! Some astonished visitors claim that they have been magnetized by the pull of the North and South poles. Others suspect that an atomic reaction has taken place." (That might explain all those hillbillies with two heads and four arms one sees lounging around their stills in the area.)

Yet another Mystery Hill could be found in Gatlinburg, next door to the Jolly Golf course, sharing a common parking lot. Perhaps it was a bit less convincing than the rest because of its nonsecluded location; despite its name, it was not even on a hill. That didn't stop people from changing size as they moved about or water from defying the law of gravity by running uphill. After Mystery Hill was leveled, its site sat dormant for many years until the Ripley's Davy Crockett Mini-Golf course was built on the land both it and Jolly Golf once occupied. Perhaps someone had better tell the golfers about that in case they wonder why their golf balls insist on rolling uphill.

No, I haven't forgotten (but you probably have) that this chapter started out talking about the museums that exhibited inanimate celebrities, such as the American Historical Wax Museum, Stars over Gatlinburg, and Ripley's Believe It or Not! Museum. The point that we were trying to make those many pages ago was that during the 1960s, real live celebrities began using the mountains as a place to hang their hats, and it is to their familiar countenances that we now turn the spotlight.

In the previous chapter, we mentioned the association between the Gold City/Lost Mine attraction in Franklin, North Carolina, and famed farmyard funnyman Archie Campbell. Campbell obviously had an affinity for East Tennessee: he was a native of the area and had gotten his start in radio on a Knoxville station. Therefore, it is not surprising that Campbell was apparently the first big-name star to set up a continuously operating show in the area.

By 1968, Gatlinburg's Heritage Hall was home to the stage show

The Mystery Hill near Blowing Rock, opened in 1948, was one of the earliest of these classic roadside "tilt houses" in the southern hills.

At Mystery Hill in Gatlinburg, girls could experience their first growth spurts and then watch water spurting uphill.

Archie Campbell brought many of his *Grand Ole Opry* cronies to Gatlinburg's Heritage Hall beginning in the mid-1960s. This ad from 1968 features the Duke of Paducah, among other performers.

billed as "Archie Campbell presents Stars of the Grand Ole Opry." It featured a consistent cast of performers, although most of them were not quite as well known as the show's title would indicate. They were a talented group nonetheless, and Campbell would join right in as part of the act whenever he was not otherwise booked. His son, Phil, was also a regular member of the cast, a job that would serve as valuable training for the future.

Aside from the Campbell clan, the most active act to host a live show in the region was Bonnie Lou and Buster. Perhaps they are not exactly household names today, but the bucolic pair was a starring feature in Knoxville's broadcasting history, and their *Smoky Mountain Hayride* shows filled the Pigeon Forge Coliseum for many years. In 1977, their show was advertised with four elements that would become the building blocks of the celebrity theater invasion to come: "country, bluegrass, gospel and clog dance."

The tourist centers served as outposts not only for Nashville and Knoxville performers but for live theater of other types. In 1977, Gatlinburg became home to the Sweet Fanny Adams Theater and Music Hall, which attempted to revive the 1890s style of entertainment in a more or less authentic fashion. The resident thespians were known as the Great Victorian Amusement Company, and they staged plays with such melodramatic titles as *Lucifer McRotten Strikes Again, or Whatever Happened to Millard Fillmore?*

Sweet Fanny Adams faced more competition than having to pay the mortgage: the Smoky Dinner Theater came to Pigeon Forge with plays carrying similar *Rocky and Bullwinkle*–style titles, such as *Virtue Rewarded: He Chased Her 'Round the Forge but She Was Nobody's Pigeon*. Closer to home in Gatlinburg, the Wonderland Cabaret let guests interact with costumed characters from *Alice in Wonderland*, no matter how curiouser and curiouser that might have seemed in a mountain resort.

Meanwhile, Archie Campbell's show that started it all just kept getting bigger and bigger. By 1978 Campbell had moved out of Heritage Hall and into Gatlinburg's Ramada Inn Convention Center. Shortly thereafter, he acquired a piece of property along Pigeon Forge's strip—which was not yet congested with other attractions—and drew up plans for his own Hee Haw Village, a miniature theme park modeled after the syndicated country comedy show for which he had become so well-known.

The building facades in Hee Haw Village were designed to look like the TV show's sets, which gave fits to the carpenters who were assigned to construct them, as nothing was supposed to be straight or level. A life-sized statue of Campbell, seated in a spring wagon and driving the *Hee Haw* logo donkey, served as a roadside lure. Although the complex contained gift shops and handicrafts, the theater was the main feature, and here Campbell continued to appear regularly

whenever he was in town. Phil Campbell, a veteran of the shows since the Heritage Hall days, demonstrated his flair for comedy as a stooge for his dad.

That comedic training came in handy after Archie Campbell died of a heart attack in 1987. Phil kept Hee Haw Village going for a few years by headlining the show himself—and in fact, he joined the cast of the *Hee Haw* television show in 1989, although he made no attempt to imitate or replace his father. At Hee Haw Village, Campbell got to experience firsthand the close connection rural comedy performers can make with their fans:

> My dad had a tradition of signing autographs until the very last person had left, and I kept that up after I started doing the show. One night I noticed a lady who was sort of hanging back until everyone else had gone, and when I asked if I could help her, she said, "I just wanted to say thank you." I said, "Well, you're welcome, but for what?" She explained that her own father had died about six months before, and that her mother had been in a deep depression ever since. The family thought that maybe a trip to the mountains would help cheer her up, but nothing had seemed to work in all the days they had been here. Finally they came to see our show, and the lady said that when they left, her mother was smiling and laughing for the first time. Well, you could have torn my heart out and stomped on it right then, I had so many tears in my eyes.

Phil Campbell turned the complex over to other interests in 1994. After a couple of false starts, the Campbell theater became home to a group known as the Comedy Barn. "At first, they did basically the same show we had been doing, with even the same band," Campbell remarks. That troupe is still performing on the same spot, although

153

Archie Campbell made it a point to remain around his theater each evening until every fan who wanted to talk to him had gone.

After Archie Campbell's death in 1987, his son, Phil, kept the show going. After passing through some ownership changes, the attraction emerged as today's Comedy Barn. The resemblance to *Hee Haw* remains quite in evidence.

the former Hee Haw Village structures were demolished long ago. The current Comedy Barn occupies only a portion of what was once Campbell's mini–theme park and is hemmed in by other development on both sides. Regardless, the show carries on with the same hokey humor that has endured for generations and will probably still be around when more sophisticated forms of humor have laughed their last.

Way back in chapter 4, we briefly discussed a couple of other live shows that enlivened things in the early 1980s. Family Showstreet USA was the rather odd name of a facility located on the Parkway in downtown Gatlinburg. It was a project of a company known as Leisure Associates, headed by Florida tourism veteran Page Robinson. His longest tenure had been as manager of R. B. Coburn's Six Gun Territory at Silver Springs, so Robinson knew his way around the tourist corral. Six Gun had gone to Boot Hill by the time Robinson took aim at Gatlinburg, and Showstreet USA wasted no effort in promoting its "three great attractions." In addition to the Disney-cloned Smoky Mountain Bear Band show mentioned earlier, the complex also featured the Musical Mountain Fountains, described as "spectacular fountains that bounce and dance to the rhythms of your favorite melodies." (This concept was not unknown in Florida either, where more than one attraction featured similar shows.) Family Showstreet USA also had the Theater of the Stars, subtitled A Tribute to Elvis. The advertising was a bit confusing, because the description underneath announced, "Beneath a 360-degree dome, lasers and thirty-two special effect projectors create a spectacular tribute to John Lennon." No matter whether the show saluted Elvis Lennon or John Presley or some mutant combination of the two, Family Showstreet USA got the hook and is barely remembered today—if at all.

A similar fate awaited Gatlinburg Place, located on Airport Road and featuring its own Disney rip-off, the Backwoods Bear Jamboree.

156

Human entertainment was spotlighted in the revue *Pop Goes America*, a typically upbeat pastiche of music and dance. Whereas Family Showstreet USA was plugging its 360-degree theater featuring some dead rock legend or another, Gatlinburg Place bragged about its IMAX theater with a seven-story-high movie screen. According to the hype, "You'll feel what it's like to fly, blast off into space, soar over treacherous mountains, plunge on a roller coaster, and marvel at some of the most beautiful scenery ever filmed." This sounds faintly reminiscent of the Flying Saucer ride at Magic World, but from this description, the IMAX film apparently did not concentrate solely on sights in the Smokies.

Whether emphasizing city slickers as Gatlinburg Place did or the rural humor of Hee Haw Village and the Comedy Barn, all of these spots looked like soggy cornflakes when compared to the celebrity theaters that arrived in the 1990s. Inspired by the success of such venues in Branson, Missouri, imposing edifices began to almost completely line the stretch of U.S. 441 from Sevierville to Pigeon Forge. Actually, Phil Campbell explained, the surface similarity did not run as deep as many people imagine. "A lot of people compare Branson to Pigeon Forge," he says, "but it's kind of like apples and oranges. I've worked in Branson, and pretty much all you have there is the theaters. If you're not there to fish or hunt, you're there to see a show. There's a whole lot more to do up here, and Branson has maybe 5 or 6 million visitors a year while the Smokies have 15 or 20 million."

The celebrities who came to dinner primarily came from the world of country music, but by that time there was so much crossover with the pop charts that it could be difficult to say just which musical genre was their true home. Lee Greenwood might have been proud to

Stars didn't get any bigger around Pigeon Forge than Dolly Parton, and theaters didn't get any bigger than her lavish Music Mansion.

Lee Greenwood and Louise Mandrell were two of the big-name celebrities who opened theaters along U.S. 441 during the 1990s.

Former circus clown Billy Baker was best known as the goofy hillbilly Elwood Smooch, but his makeup kit also contained other faces and personalities.

be an American, but he was also proud to set up shop in Sevierville. Louise Mandrell left her sisters Barbara and Irlene to fend for themselves and moved into a theater in the neighborhood. The group Alabama did not actually hang out in Tennessee, but their namesake Alabama Grill served up its grub within a museum of their mementoes. *Grand Ole Opry* stars Jim Ed Brown and Helen Cornelius harmonized at the Eagle Mountain Theater, with magician Terry Evanswood thrown into the mix. Even Anita Bryant, well remembered for her many years as the queen of Florida orange juice, squeezed out a few more pennies in a huge building that was formerly Dolly Parton's Music Mansion.

While the names and faces changed, the advertising for all of these shows makes them sound like kissin' cousins. They all combined modern country music with southern gospel singing, interspersed with humor of a type only slightly less corny than *Hee Haw* and unflaggingly featuring patriotic numbers guaranteed to get the audience to its feet.

For some reason, this celebrity theater boom lasted for only about a decade, after which the stars all went back to whatever firmament they had come from. Louise Mandrell was the holdout, hanging on until New Year's Eve 2005. Most of the theaters are still there and playing to packed houses, but with headliners that do not depend so much on their name value. The Black Bear Jamboree continued the country/gospel/comedy/patriotic quartet of winning formats. The Country Tonite Theater did the same and gave Terry Evanswood a place to hang his magic hat after the Eagle Mountain Theater had flown away. The American Jukebox Theater lit up with an eclectic playlist that ranged from "At the Hop" and "Chapel of Love" to "Man, I Feel Like a Woman" and "Coal Miner's Daughter." Dolly Parton parlayed the success of her theme park into a chain of Dixie Stampede dinner theaters—including one in Pigeon Forge—although she was not a part of the show. The Ole Smoky Hoedown show was a country clone of the Comedy Barn, starring rubber-faced hillbilly comic Elwood Smooch. In real life, Elwood was Billy Baker, an inductee into the International Clown Hall of Fame who had once auditioned to become the world's most famous clown, Bozo.

A quick survey in the autumn of 2005 also turned up theaters known as Fiddler's Feast, the Classic Country Theater, the Governor's Palace, Great China Acrobats, Smoky Mountain Jubilee, and the Memories Theater, which built its whole reputation around a salute to Elvis (what, no John Lennon impersonators?). The dinner theater concept apparently has come to town to stay, and even if the headliners are no longer as luminous as those from the 1990s, they still seem to be giving visitors exactly what they want, and plenty of it.

SEVEN

Look Out, Lookout Mountain

In all the pages that have preceded this one, it might have seemed that we were deliberately overlooking one gigantic concentration of mountain attractions. Well, the fact is that we were ignoring it on purpose, but for good reason. Lookout Mountain, the southern end of what is normally considered the Land of the Smokies, became basically a tourism world of its own, isolated from the others but drawing much of its business from travelers heading either to or from the rest of the Tennessee and North Carolina mountain country. Incidentally, it is almost useless to try to designate what state hosted any particular Lookout Mountain attraction, as the Tennessee-Georgia boundary sliced right through them. Chattanooga was the main jumping-off point for Lookout's sights, so we shall leave it at that and let Rand McNally buffs hash it out from there.

In the 1890s, Lookout Mountain was still primarily a residential area, and it required a strong constitution to even try to make one's home there. The families living on Lookout included the Carters, and Garnet and Paul Carter would have a lot to do with developing the spot for tourists. In 1974, Paul Carter reminisced about life on Lookout in the early days:

> At this time only one road served the mountain, it being a very poor toll road. Now, having been greatly improved, it is

It had long been reported that on a clear day, visitors to Umbrella Rock could see parts of seven states.

During the 1920s, Lookout Mountain began moving from a primarily residential area to a true tourist destination.

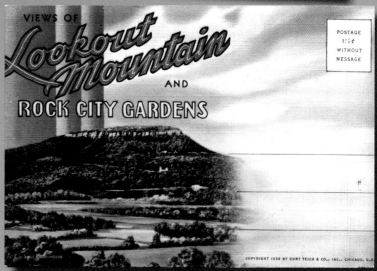

VIEWS OF

Lookout Mountain

AND

ROCK CITY GARDENS

called the Ochs Highway. By the latter part of the 1890s, Lookout Mountain began coming into its own. Lookout Inn, a 400-room hotel, was built across from the present Incline Station, and the present Incline and a broad-gauge steam engine track was built from St. Elmo to the top of the mountain. The railroad was a great factor in the growth of the Mountain, hauling building materials, coal, and such. All the hotels and a college on the mountain were eventually destroyed by fire and not rebuilt.

Living on the mountain in those days was quite crude. There were no hard-surfaced roads, no running water in homes, and houses were poorly sealed. In the winter the rooms were quite cold, warmed either by grate fireplaces or stoves. . . . All homes had privies located in the back yards. Conveyance was by horse and buggy or wagon. There were no telephones or fire departments.

Tourism might have been slow in coming, especially under the primitive living conditions Carter described, but it was nevertheless creeping in, almost unnoticed. The first Lookout Mountain Incline began hauling visitors up the side in 1887. Lookout had one of its earliest tourist attractions in Natural Bridge Park, which featured oddball rock formations. Nearby, Umbrella Rock was another outcropping from which it had been claimed for years that one could see into seven states (Georgia, Tennessee, Alabama, North and South Carolina, Kentucky, and Virginia, which not coincidentally comprised the South's entire mountain tourism industry).

The Civil War battle site on Lookout's northernmost extremity was dedicated as Point Park in 1898. That same year, the Spanish-American War broke out, and fifty thousand Army troops were stationed at nearby Chickamauga Park in Georgia. Not only did these soldiers bring more money into the area, but their visiting families became tourists as well. Future tourism tycoon Garnet Carter was on hand in 1899, operating a souvenir stand at the park. It was a business he would come to know intimately.

After working at several other jobs that honed his salesmanship skills to a razor-sharp edge, in 1924 Carter decided to create his own version of the land boom that was exploding down in Florida. He bought up three hundred acres of ground on the very top of Lookout Mountain and announced his plans to build a residential development. Because his wife, Frieda, had an undying interest in ancient European fairy tales, Carter named his new neighborhood Fairyland and gave all of the streets suitable names: Red Riding Hood Trail, Peter Pan Road, and so forth. The development was decorated with imported German statues of elves, gnomes, and assorted folktale characters that fit the prevailing theme.

164

The Fairyland neighborhood on Lookout Mountain featured imported German statues of famous folklore characters, such as these renditions of Little Red Riding Hood and her wolfish companion.

The year after the Fairyland neighborhood was opened, Carter did himself one better by building a luxury hotel, the Fairyland Inn. Not to be outdone, in 1928 his brother, Paul, built the even larger Lookout Mountain Hotel a few miles away, and the brethren became cheerful rivals. A Chattanooga newspaper writer described their good-natured game of one-upmanship:

> These boys can help each other out. You see, if Paul has a house full of guests and Garnet wants some of them, Garnet can go up to Paul's hotel and try to sell his guests a lot. They will all get mad and go to Fairyland. Then Garnet can follow them down to his hotel and tell them if they don't buy a lot he will throw them out. You see, they have no other place to go.
>
> These Carter brothers are figuring on making the old Johnson Pike a one-way road next summer, and that will be going up. Once on the mountain, you will be there all season. If they go down on the Incline, Garnet and Paul will have their automobile for the first payment on the lot.
>
> Garnet says he will furnish the bus line for his little brother Paul. Garnet plans to have his bus run out of gas at Fairyland and unload all the fine feathered birds from up north, then take all the pelicans from Florida up to Paul's hotel. Paul says he won't need any writing paper, for he is going to make everyone pay cash in advance. He won't have to send out any bills, and all his guests will be having so much fun they won't want to write home. Garnet says all his guests, after he gets through with them, won't have enough money to write home.

Yes, spirits were high atop Lookout Mountain. Garnet Carter soon came up with another idea that would not only please the guests at his hotel but also become a national craze. In front of the Fairyland

When Garnet and Frieda Carter installed a game they called Tom Thumb Golf at their Fairyland Inn, they created the first true miniature golf course. (Rock City Collection)

The stone blasted out of the mountain to create Ruby Falls's elevator shaft was used to construct this distinctive entrance building, which opened in 1930.

The cave containing Ruby Falls was originally one of two Lookout Mountain caverns opened to the public.

See **RUBY FALLS** in Lookout Mountain *Caves*

AAA

Ruby Falls 145 ft. HIGH *and* 1120 ft. UNDERGROUND

CHATTANOOGA, TENN.

Inn he constructed a putting green decorated with fanciful statues and with hazards through which the golf balls had to be maneuvered. Practically without intending to do so, Carter had invented the game of miniature golf. Similar concepts had previously existed, but they had all been used primarily as a substitute or practice run for genuine golf courses. Carter not only patented his game but franchised it nationwide as Tom Thumb Golf.

Fads such as miniature golf came in handy after the stock market crash in October 1929. The wealthy tourists who had comprised Lookout Mountain's clientele suddenly were too busy jumping out of windows to make the trip to the luxury hotels. Paul Carter's Lookout Mountain Hotel closed for good, and it now serves as the central building of Covenant College. The Fairyland Inn also went to Never-Never Land, although in 1934 it was reorganized as a private country club for residents of the mountain, and it remains so today.

Other events were also taking place that would help turn Lookout into a hangout for the general tourist public. In 1928, spelunker Leo Lambert conceived the idea of opening an old cave at the base of the mountain as an attraction; he obtained some property on the mountainside and began drilling an elevator shaft. Before reaching the intended cave, however, the workers unexpectedly broke through into another cave located above the one they were seeking. This cave turned out to contain a spectacular underground waterfall, which Lambert named Ruby Falls in honor of his wife. Stone removed during the drilling of the elevator shaft was used to construct an elaborate entrance building, which became known as Cavern Castle. Ruby Falls formally opened to the public on June 16, 1930.

For several years, visitors to Ruby Falls had a choice about which cave they wanted to visit. The elevator shaft went all the way down to the much larger cavern at the bottom, where relics indicated that Confederate troops had headquartered during the Civil War. Ruby

Falls's management never failed to point out the alleged signature of Andrew Jackson on the cave wall (making him the first graffiti artist in the South?). However, for all its historic value, the lower cave lacked the majestic stalactite and stalagmite formations found in the smaller cave—and of course, it also did not have Ruby Falls. Since virtually no one chose to visit the lower cave, tours to that level were discontinued in 1935, and all the publicity centered on the waterfall level.

To this day, debate continues about just how much of Ruby Falls's water flow is genuine and how much is augmented to make it more impressive. Tourists really do not seem to care either way. Approaching the falls in total darkness has been a high point of many vacations, with the mystical strains of Richard Strauss's "Also Sprach Zarathustra" rumbling over the loudspeakers until the final thunderous chord, signaling the multicolored lighting to illuminate Ruby Falls in all its glory.

Meanwhile, back in Fairyland, Garnet Carter was looking for a way to make a living now that his hotel had gone the way of the stock market. The answer seemed to lie in the piece of property he had retained for himself while selling lots in Fairyland. The acreage was strewn with rock formations of incredible size and variety and situated in such a way as to afford narrow pathways between them. Since the early 1800s, this part of Lookout Mountain had been known as the "rock city," and after Fairyland opened to visitors and residents, Frieda Carter had noticed their interest in exploring the rocks. With the encouragement of her husband, Garnet, Frieda set out to create the rock garden to end all rock gardens.

With the help of some interested friends, Frieda began the commercial development of Rock City. She took some string and marked a trail leading to the large rock outcropping known variously as Lover's Leap and Steamer Rock (because of its resemblance to the prow

ROCK CITY
GARDENS
Atop Lookout Mountain
CHATTANOOGA, TENNESSEE

SEE SEVEN STATES

EE RUBY FALLS

CLOCKWISE FROM LEFT:

Rock City Gardens welcomed its first visitors in May 1932. It would become Lookout Mountain's biggest tourist attraction.

The colorful lights that illuminated Ruby Falls would be lit on the final note of "Also Sprach Zarathustra" (better known as the theme from *2001: A Space Odyssey*).

For years, Ruby Falls's distinctive green and white billboards were common sights along the South's highways. This, one of the final surviving examples, was photographed in 1992.

The Enchanted Trail IN ROCK

HOME OF
MR. & MRS. GARNET CARTER

UP THROUGH
PAST NEE

LOVERS' LEAP
A WONDERFUL VIEW OF
7 STATES -- KENTUCKY, VIRGINIA,
TENNESSEE, GEORGIA, ALABAMA,
NORTH AND SOUTH CAROLINA

TORTOISE SHELL
ROCK

DOWN THROU
FAT MAN'S SQU

CAVE OF
THE WINDS

1000-TON
BALANCED ROCK

GARDENS

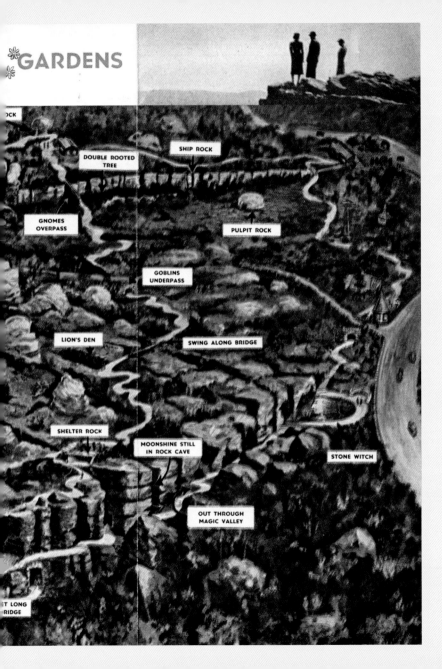

Rock City's "Enchanted Trail" wound around rock formations and through crevices, passing many gnomes and other statues that had originally adorned the Fairyland neighborhood.

DOUBLE ROOTED TREE

SHIP ROCK

GNOMES OVERPASS

PULPIT ROCK

GOBLINS UNDERPASS

LION'S DEN

SWING ALONG BRIDGE

SHELTER ROCK

MOONSHINE STILL IN ROCK CAVE

STONE WITCH

OUT THROUGH MAGIC VALLEY

of a ship jutting out from the mountainside). As mentioned earlier in the discussion of Blowing Rock, the world of roadside attractions is liberally spiced with legends involving people—usually Indians, who should have known better from all the years they spent in the wilderness—leaping off cliffs either to meet a spectacular demise or to be rescued by supernatural forces. Rock City's Lover's Leap fell into the former category. The tale that explained its origin first appeared in print in 1876:

> The tradition runs that Sautee was a brave of a tribe between which and the Cherokees a deadly feud existed. Upon some occasion he saw the beautiful daughter of the chief of the Cherokees, Nacoochee, the "Evening Star." With the ardent Sautee, to see was to love her.
>
> As no concession on the part of her father could be expected, she eloped with her lover. She not only sacrificed all the sweet charities of home and kindred friends and country, but the opposition to the match being so great in Sautee's tribe as her own, she could find no shelter with her husband's people. In the extremity they took shelter in a cave in the rock-ribbed sides of Lookout Mountain.
>
> The angry father of the "Evening Star" had vowed vengeance against Sautee and he found many anxious and disappointed young braves to aid in his search. At length Sautee was found, attacked and overpowered by numbers and taken prisoner. He was condemned to death by being thrown from the precipice of Lookout and all the tribe was gathered on top of the mountain to witness the sacrifice. Nacoochee was forced to be present to witness the death of him she loved better than life. With a voice loud and clear as a battle cry, he sang his death song.

The most famous sight in Rock City was Lover's Leap, which lifted Umbrella Rock's claim of a view into seven states.

The rocks still gave back the echo of the mournful cadence when two strong braves seized him in their arms, raised him high in the air, and flung him far over the precipice. While the attention of the tribe was absorbed in this tragedy, Nacoochee seized the opportunity of their negligence and sprang over the precipice.

One hundred feet below, all that remained of the devoted lovers was found stilled in death. With a heart filled with grief and remorse, the stricken father buried them side by side in the lovely valley.

On Frieda Carter's original Rock City trail, reaching this legendary spot for leaping lovers called for a rather strenuous climb around the formation's back side. To make the location more accessible to the average tourist, Fairyland employee Don Gault devised a swinging bridge built of leftover cables from the Incline. The trail was surfaced with pine needles and pebble gravel. Frieda collected wildflowers and other plants and had them replanted along her trail. The total effect was such that it appeared the flowers had always grown there, and to this day many people are prone to forget that Rock City Gardens is indeed a garden in every sense of the word. Many of the gnomes and statues of storybook characters that had populated the Fairyland neighborhood and the Tom Thumb Golf course were carted to Rock City and placed into new surroundings.

Although the property was left in its natural state as much as possible, a few "improvements" on Mother Nature were made. A crevice underneath a large overhanging rock was filled in to make a floor, and the resulting grotto was dubbed Shelter Rock. Some passageways were widened slightly to make the path easier to navigate, and other passageways were blasted through the solid rock to make shortcuts.

It is easy to forget that Rock City Gardens is indeed a garden in every sense of the word, because the flowers and other plants were placed so skillfully that they appeared always to have been there.

Shelter Rock had no floor under it until Rock City's operators filled in the crevasse during the early days.

A small, round building with a conical roof was built at the entrance to the gardens. Known as the Sugar Loaf Shop, the tiny structure doubled as an office for Frieda Carter and a souvenir stand. Rock City Gardens welcomed its first visitors on May 21, 1932.

While attendance during those first years was reasonable, Carter felt that more people really should be coming through the gates. Location was part of the problem: while Rock City's perch on top of the mountain was a fine thing for a view of seven states, it also meant that people were not just going to pass by and decide to stop on a whim. They had to be made aware that Rock City was there. Enter Clark Byers.

The twenty-one-year-old Byers had worked at a variety of odd jobs before joining Chattanooga's Southern Ad Company, a sign-painting firm. His wages of seven dollars per week were such an increase over what he had been making at his previous jobs that he frequently found himself working through his lunch breaks, overwhelmed by his enthusiasm.

Fred Maxwell, a good friend of Garnet Carter, was Byers's boss and did not ignore his zeal. One day in 1936, Maxwell asked his enthusiastic young employee to come along for a drive. "I didn't know where we were going," Byers later recalled, "but we got to talking about painting ads on barn roofs, and Mr. Maxwell said, 'If I ever get Garnet Carter started on barn roofs, he'll paint them till his whiskers get down to his belt.'"

Maxwell introduced Byers to Carter, and the three of them agreed that Byers would paint barn roofs with Rock City advertisements at forty dollars per roof. The first barn painted by Byers was located near Kimball, Tennessee, on U.S. Highway 41 (known as the Dixie Highway because it was the primary route used by tourists traveling from Chicago to Florida). Unlike the famous barn roofs to come, the original sign had a red background with white letters and spelled out 35 MILES TO ROCK CITY ATOP LOOKOUT MOUNTAIN.

Clark Byers began painting barn roofs with Rock City signage in 1936. After many years of neglect, a number of the surviving signs have been painstakingly restored

Since Rock City generally used the barn roof, other area attractions—in this case, Wonder Cave at Monteagle—sometimes used the structure's walls.

The popular public image is that of a barn roof painted with the three words SEE ROCK CITY. In actuality, that particular combination was rarely used alone. Embellishment was common, and Byers's signs ran the gamut from SEE BEAUTIFUL ROCK CITY to SEE ROCK CITY, WORLD'S EIGHTH WONDER and later to more elaborate aphorisms such as WHEN YOU SEE ROCK CITY YOU SEE THE BEST and 'TWOULD BE A PITY TO MISS ROCK CITY. In the meantime, Byers had discovered that black paint was much less expensive than red, and his roofs became black with white letters, a color combination that would dominate Rock City's advertising in all media for the next fifty years.

The barns covered the United States as far west as Texas and as far north as Lansing, Michigan. They became an integral part of the American roadside scene and gave Rock City the boost it needed. With Rock City, Ruby Falls, and Point Park drawing more tourists up the mountain's roads, a curious business developed down below. Although nearly forgotten today, a large factor in the area's tourism industry was the Lookout Mountain guides. Stationed in booths at the foot of the mountain, the guides (for a fee, of course) would take the wheel of tourists' cars and handle the driving to the various attractions. The attractions would in turn pay the guides a percentage of their profits.

The guides often used scare tactics to convince tourists that the guides' expertise was vital. In particular, the guides would prey on cars with license plates from flatland states, solemnly stating that the roads on Lookout Mountain were far too dangerous for strangers to attempt on their own. There were no set guide fees—the guides would charge excessive amounts to visitors they judged to be more prosperous. Then, even though attractions such as Rock City and Ruby Falls were paying commissions, the guides would sometimes bypass these places to get back to the foot of the mountain as soon as possible and pick up another carload of tourists.

Lookout Mountain
INCLINE
RAILWAY

The Steepest and Safest Passenger Incline in the World.
Chattanooga, Tennessee

1. GRAND CORRIDOR
2. SNOW WHITE
3. SHIP ROCK
4. DOUBLE-ROOTED TREE
5. NEEDLE'S EYE
6. DEER PARK
MUSHROOM ROCK
8. GNOMES OVER-PASS
9. GOBLINS UNDER-PASS
10. SHELTER ROCK

YOU DON'T NEED A ROADSIDE GUIDE TO SEE

Drive Your Own Car
The Easily Driven Scenic

11. SWING-ALONG BRI
13. LOVER'S LEAP
15. TORTOISE SHELL R
17. 1,000-TON BALANCE
19. OBSERVATION POIN

K CITY GARDENS
d Follow HIGHWAY 58
hway Up Lookout Mountain

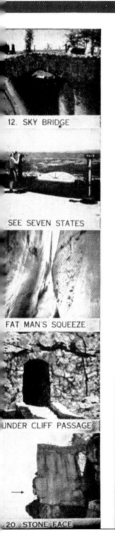

12. SKY BRIDGE

SEE SEVEN STATES

FAT MAN'S SQUEEZE

UNDER CLIFF PASSAGE

20. STONE FACE

21. RAINBOW HALL

22. DRAGON'S CAVE

23. UNDER CLIFF TUNNEL

24. CAVE OF THE WINDS

25 HALL OF THE MOUNTAIN KING

26. MOONSHINE STILL

27. STONE WITCH

28. MAGIC VALLEY

29. LITTLE RED RIDING HOOD

30. PULPIT ROCK

FAR LEFT: Although the Lookout Mountain Incline had been running since 1887, it fell into disuse until it was revived as a tourist attraction in the 1930s. Today, it retains its appeal to tourists but is also part of Chattanooga's mass transit system.

LEFT: The wording at the top of this late 1930s brochure has no special significance unless one is aware of the power struggle then going on between Rock City and the Lookout Mountain guides extorting money from the area's attractions.

179

In 1947, construction began on Fairyland Caverns, which would prove to be Rock City's largest man-made addition.

In October 1937, Garnet Carter announced that he was going to take over operation of the creaky old Lookout Mountain Incline, which had fallen almost into disuse since the arrival of the automobile. The fact that the Incline would once again be available to haul tourists up the mountain did not sit well with the guides, who declared war on Garnet Carter and Rock City. In the beginning, the management at Ruby Falls sided with the guides. Owner Shirmer Brown stated that he believed that Carter's charges against the guides were "vicious and unjust," and he praised the guides as public-spirited. Boasted one of the most public-spirited guides, "We took three customers away from Rock City today, and when the weather is good we will be taking eight customers a day." Brown and Ruby Falls abruptly switched allegiance when it became evident that Carter had local government on his side. Point Park, the mountain's third big draw, remained above the fray since it charged no admission fee and so could pay no commissions.

The guides tried every form of dirty pool to keep people away from Rock City and Ruby Falls, including one nefarious plot to steer tourists away from Chattanooga by claiming that the city was infested with fleas, but their reign of terror ended when World War II temporarily stemmed the flow of tourists. The guide business did not survive to see the new postwar world, but when families started hitting the road again, Rock City had big plans to welcome them.

Although his inspiration remains unknown, immediately after the war, Garnet Carter conceived the idea of an entire series of fairy tale scenes to be placed in a man-made cave he would call Fairyland Caverns, the culmination, perhaps, of all the development that had already gone into the Fairyland community and Tom Thumb Golf. It was, to all appearances, the first of the many fairy-tale-themed attractions that would become such a large part of baby boomer tourism.

Before construction began, the part of Rock City that is now Fairyland Caverns resembled a longer, wider version of the park's famed Fat Man's Squeeze. Workmen widened this existing crevice and put a roof over it, while the ornate Red Riding Hood sign that had once adorned the entrance to the Fairyland neighborhood was placed over the doorway.

While these plans were germinating, Carter had become acquainted with a talented husband-and-wife team of sculptors from Atlanta, Charles and Jessie Sanders, and he now enlisted their help in turning Fairyland Caverns into more than just a dream world. No one today really knows how Carter arrived at the idea of illuminating his Fairyland Caverns scenes with ultraviolet light (black light). He may or may not have seen black light used in amusement park fun houses (which eventually evolved into dark rides of the type visited earlier in our discussions of Magic World and Silver Dollar City), but he knew that he wanted it to be a part of his beloved Fairyland Caverns. The glowing color effect produced by black light proved quite a novelty for those who had not encountered it before.

Jessie Sanders never used a sketch pad to plan her figures ahead of time, as she preferred to work straight from her imagination. She studied the ragamuffin appearance of late 1940s' war orphans to get the pathos necessary for Hansel and Gretel; an illustration in a coloring book inspired the "witchy tree" that loomed behind the two children. When sculpting the figure of Cinderella fleeing from the ball at midnight, Sanders posed in front of a mirror to get the position of the hands just the way she wanted. Garnet Carter suggested that the first scene be a mother reading bedtime stories to her children and that the second scene depict the children asleep in bed as their "dream fairies" floated through an open window.

Since all of Fairyland Caverns was not completed at the same time, its opening date is somewhat vague. Work on it began in earnest in 1947. August 1948 newspaper articles mentioned the Caverns as Rock City's newest attraction, but more than a year later, in October 1949, other articles referred to it as having just been completed. In any case, it was a huge hit among tourists and their baby boomer kiddies, so much so that in 1964, Sanders added Mother Goose Village, a room-sized diorama depicting intermingled scenes from the most beloved nursery rhymes, again illuminated under black light. Sanders remained on staff until her retirement in 1968, after which her creations were left in the capable hands of successors who respectfully maintain them to this day.

Another of the people most responsible for Rock City's success left the company that same year, but for a totally different reason. Clark Byers was still on the road, although by now his work mainly involved repainting existing signs rather than creating new ones. In 1968 he went to retouch a Rock City sign on U.S. 41, about seven miles east of Murfreesboro, Tennessee, and received quite a shock— literally. Climbing up to the sign, he noticed that the paint had done an unusual amount of peeling in one particular spot. Byers couldn't figure out why at first, but he soon found out the reason. The wind from a passing truck blew some low-hanging power lines against the

Jessie Sanders added Mother Goose Village to Fairyland Caverns in 1964.

metal sign, sending seventy-two hundred volts of electricity through Byers's body. His hair was ablaze and his left side was totally paralyzed, but he managed to hold on to his perch with his right hand while his assistant, who had been standing on the ground and was not injured, could get him down and to a hospital.

Although Byers later recovered with no appreciable aftereffects, the accident closed the chapter on the original Rock City sign painter. By that point, the growth of the interstate highway system, combined with the attempts at highway beautification spearheaded by the president's wife, Lady Bird Johnson, had caused many of the Rock City barns to be either demolished or painted over. Fortunately for the few that remained, the 1990s brought a renewed appreciation for roadside nostalgia, and several of them have now been restored to their former glory.

An interesting bit of trivia regarding the Lookout Mountain attractions is how often they made the scene in the pop music charts. Of course, the Smokies and their immediate vicinity were indirectly referenced in such hits as Lester Flatt and Earl Scruggs's "Foggy Mountain Breakdown" and in that celebration of hillbilly culture,

This is Your Guide Through
BEAUTIFUL ROCK CITY

atop Lookout Mountain near Chattanooga, Tenn.

HELLO there! These pictures of some of the outstanding attractions in Rock City are arranged as you will come to them. When you finish your tour, you may want to send this to one of your friends back home.

Rocky

4. Mushroom Rock

8. High Falls

3. Deer Park

7. Swing-Along Bridge

2. Needle's Eye

6. Shelter Rock

1. Grand Corridor

5. Goblin's Underpass

9. Lover's Leap
10. See Seven States
11. Fat Man's Squeeze
12. 1000-Ton Balanced Rock
13. Observation Point
14. Moonshine Still
15. Entrance to Fairyland Caverns
16. Hansel and Grethel
17. Cinderella
18. Mother Goose Village
19. Little Bo-Peep
20. Rub-Adub-Dub

For your own safety and for the preservation of the beauty and charm of ROCK CITY – PLEASE STAY IN THE TRAIL!

Rock City's standard guide card from the late 1960s and 1970s spelled out twenty of the high points visitors would encounter along the Enchanted Trail.

The Confederama, at the base of Lookout Mountain, re-created the Civil War battles of the area on a miniature landscape.

"Rocky Top, Tennessee" (reportedly composed by Boudleaux and Felice Bryant in a room at the Gatlinburg Inn hotel in 1965). And we should not forget Ronnie Milsap's 1980 hit "Smoky Mountain Rain," in which Gatlinburg made a single appearance in one line. However, for specific attractions being mentioned by name, even Gatlinburg had to bow to Lookout Mountain.

In late 1951, Tennessee Ernie Ford and the Denning Sisters released the "Rock City Boogie." It had a catchy tune and lyrics that began, "Atop Lookout Mountain, up in Chattanooga / Everybody's doin' the Rock City Boogie." Rock City was also mentioned, in company with Ruby Falls, in Tabby West's 1955 single, "Chat-Chat-Chat-tanooga." Rural comedian Bob Corley had an early 1960s hit with his comedy monologue "Number One Street" (aka U.S. Highway 1), which contained references to Rock City as well as Silver Springs, Stuckey's, and other southern roadside fixtures.

With the pesky Lookout Mountain guides a thing of the past, the 1950s and 1960s saw other attractions spring up like daffodils around the base of the summit. The Confederama came to town in 1957. Although originally located in Tiftonia, Georgia, it soon moved around to the more populated side of the mountain and took its stand to live or die in Dixie. As with several other attractions discussed in this book, the Confederama brought its re-created Civil War battles to life on a miniature landscape, with animated figures acting out the battles of Chattanooga, Chickamauga, and Lookout Mountain.

Meanwhile, the chief executives of the Confederacy's nemesis were saluted at the Hall of Presidents Wax Museum, located next to the Incline's lower station. Little is known about this obscure attraction; its owner, Shelby Boyd, transferred his allegiance to Gatlinburg in 1971, opening the Hillbilly Golf course there. The small incline that

The Lookout Mountain Museum at Point Park featured realistic dioramas of key points in the mountain's history; they were created by Jessie Sanders, who was also responsible for Fairyland Caverns at Rock City.

188

took miniature golfers (and their parents) from the parking lot to the course itself was no doubt inspired by the wax museum's proximity to Lookout Mountain's railway.

Back up at Point Park, the Lookout Mountain Museum exhibited relics and artifacts from the area's battles. To depict scenes that could not easily be illustrated by such items, the museum enlisted the help of Jessie Sanders to create dioramas that stood in stark, realistic contrast to her fanciful creations in Fairyland Caverns. The Confederama and the Lookout Mountain Museum would eventually conflate: in 1994, Rock City purchased the Confederama and changed its name to the more politically correct Battles for Chattanooga Museum. In 1997, the animated landscape was removed and relocated to the Lookout Mountain Museum, essentially creating one attraction out of the remnants of two.

Today, Lookout Mountain remains a vital part of the area's tourist industry. Although somewhat separated from the rest of the South's hill country attractions, its unique concentration of various styles of tourism have given it a reputation as large as the bulk of the mountain itself.

G-260 Mountain View Hotel, Gatlinburg, Tennessee

Photo by Paul A. Moore of Tenn. Conservation Dept.

Although the Mountain View Hotel in Gatlinburg was originally built as a getaway for the wealthy, this postcard obviously comes from a later era, when the more common variety of tourist had overrun the property. (Warren Reed Collection)

EIGHT

Sleep Like a Bear

All of the attractions, shows and excitement we have visited to this point would be enough to make even the hardiest soul start yawning for the nearest comfortable bed. We will now cast a longing glance at some of the places where pooped-out tourists could rest their weary bones before closing with some miscellaneous data on the tourism industry's ongoing efforts to keep the mountains at the forefront of everyone's mind.

Inasmuch as the Great Smokies originally became a place for the wealthy to get away from it all, most of the early accommodations were built with that clientele in mind. The Mountain View Hotel was an early example, followed closely by the Riverside Hotel, Gatlinburg Inn, and Hotel Greystone. The Greystone's description of its amenities vividly painted a picture of a resort for the idle rich: "Artistically designed, in dignified stone, it is one of the South's truly beautiful hotels. Heavily wooded hills are its background, while in front lies a wide and spacious lawn, all terraced and landscaped for beauty and enjoyment. Here you can lounge about as you wish, enjoying a grand view of the Great Smokies, sun-bathing or hiking over private trails that reach the top of the hotel's 50-acre mountain property in the rear. Guides are available for fishing or hiking, anywhere you care to go."

The National Park Service was quick to point out in its brochures that accommodations within the boundaries of the Great Smoky

By some accounts, the Rocky Waters Court was the first motor court in Gatlinburg. It would not be the last.

Mountains National Park were limited to free campgrounds, the LeConte Lodge atop Mount LeConte (accessible only by foot or horseback, which would most definitely limit the amount of luggage guests could bring), and the Wonderland Hotel at Elkmont. The Wonderland originally was not a luxury resort but instead provided housing for the area's bustling lumber trade. After the last lumberjack had yelled "Timber," some of the Knoxville elite had purchased the Wonderland (with no Alice aforethought) and turned it into a spot for their own brand of mad tea parties. Many years later, the Park Service announced that no leases on Park lands would be extended past 1992, so on November 15 of that year, it was off with its head for the Wonderland. Undaunted, manager Darrell Huskey built the New Wonderland Hotel nearby, modeled as closely as possible after the original, and was open in time for the spring 1993 tourist season.

As with other forms of tourism, business owners soon discovered that common, everyday tourists greatly outnumbered the high and

These three establishments illustrate some of the many different types of Gatlinburg accommodations. King's Cabins (center) retained its original signage even after a modern motel was added.

mighty, so less luxurious facilities began to appear. With the thousands of motel rooms available in the Gatlinburg/Pigeon Forge/Cherokee environs today, it would seem impossible to pinpoint just which came first. One historian came up with the Rocky Waters Court as being Gatlinburg's first tourist cabins, dating to 1932. After that, the picture gets mighty crowded, so rather than trying to enumerate them all, it is probably best for our purposes to just mention some of the more unusual—or, for that matter, usual—entries in the room rat race.

Following the Rocky Waters's flow, many of the pre–World War II cabin courts in Gatlinburg went for the rustic log cabin look. This was exemplified by such cozy quarters as Bohanan's Tourist Rooms and Cabins and Ogle's Creek Bend Cabins. An exception to this perceived rule was Marshall's Creek Rest Court, with cabins constructed of natural stone rather than logs.

Occasionally, a cabin court would survive long enough to become a sort of cabin/motel hybrid, as in the case of King's Cabins, which kept its original neon signage for the cabins alongside its more modern name, King's Motel. Another interesting phenomenon from this period is that instead of referring to the town simply as Gatlinburg, many brochures and postcards sought out a somewhat British-sounding name and called the community Gatlinburg-in-the-Smokies.

Following only slightly behind the log cabin look—or perhaps going hand in dirty hand with it—were the motels that subscribed to the love-it-or-hate-it hillbilly theme so prevalent in the area. The community of Townsend, where Wilson's Hillbilly Restaurant was already perpetuating stereotypes of the Snuffy Smith and Li'l Abner tradition, even had one motel that called itself the Hillbilly Hilton. In Gatlinburg, Ogle's Twin Islands Motel advertised itself with a brochure written almost totally in a comedic rural dialect:

There is 20 of the most moderne units you ever did see—a couple old ones we save fer our enemies—an' some new ones to cum! We ain't kiddin' when we say these units is purty! Pigeon River seenry ain't to be sneezed at anytime early spring into late fall, and this little ole rocky mountin streem gurgles right by yer screened winders or yer doah. Crost ventilation, mountin air conditioned, handmade furniture (solid cherry), seprate dressin' rooms, dark red, tobacker brown, some green we had left over, make a restfull color scheme. Mighty comfortable beds, stuft easy chairs, lamps, big, big mirrors, rugs, ashtrays, coffee table, even a water pitcher an' some of them steerelized drinkin' glasses is all included.

On the outskirts of Asheville, the Mountaineer Inn motel didn't pull any punches when it came to heapin' helpins of its hospitality—hillbilly, that is. This establishment must have set some sort of record for depicting cartoon hillbillies not with paint but with citified neon. The roadside sign sported a gun-totin' patriarch of gigantic proportions, and the entire roofline was crowned with his neon kinfolk. Among the generic figures was one that was so familiar as to seem positively out of place: a neon rendering of Li'l Abner's feisty Mammy Yokum, although no other members of the comic strip clan were in sight.

Even more common than the hillbilly theme was the use of bears in motel advertising. As discussed earlier, bears were the unofficial trademark of the national park, and their predilection for sleeping gave them a natural association with motels and their amenities. The Bearskin Motel advertised for years with a photo someone had taken that showed two of the park bears apparently waltzing with each other: the caption read, "You'll feel like doing a dance too when you visit your Smokies!"

For unashamed usage of hillbilly stereotypes, one had to look no further than the Mountaineer Inn in Asheville. Even Li'l Abner's Mammy Yokum made a cameo appearance, separated from the rest of the comic strip cast (Warren Reed Collection).

Bears could take many forms on motel signage, from the humanized Sleepy Bear Motel logo to the fairly realistic one atop the Bear's Den Motel sign.

Perhaps none of the motels encapsulated the theme as well as the Sleepy Bear Motel, whose signage was complete with a snoozin' bruin. (The name obviously paid no heed to the California-based TraveLodge chain, which had two Gatlinburg locations by 1972. The chain's emblem was a Sleepy Bear character dressed in nightgown and nightcap.) The Smoky Cub Motor Court in Sevierville went for a similarly nonthreatening logo. The Bears' Den Motel, Bearland Court, and Bear-Land Motel used more realistic portrayals. Even the most famous Park Service resident of all, Yogi Bear, came to the area when an outlet of the chain of Jellystone Park campgrounds brought its pic-a-nic baskets to Cherokee.

Speaking of Cherokee, in that vicinity, it was of course Indian imagery that ruled the reservation when it came to motels. One of the earliest to go all out for this theme apparently was Mac's Indian Village, reportedly built in 1934, a year after the establishment of the Wigwam Village motel near Mammoth Cave, Kentucky, which had tourist cabins in the form of giant concrete tepees. Six more Wigwam Villages opened across the country during the next twenty years. It is somewhat surprising that this chain did not move into the Smokies at some point; the nearest they came was a planned location at Natural Bridge, Virginia, in 1940, but it never opened.

Mac's Indian Village took the Wigwam Village concept but used it more for strictly cosmetic purposes. The cabins were ordinary, with four walls and a roof, but each one was fronted with the metal facade of a tepee (or wigwam, or whatever the correct term may be). Some glowing touches of neon must have made the entire complex a sight to see after dark. After operating for nearly sixty years, Mac's was closed and up for sale in November 2005, and it has likely gone on to the happy hunting grounds. Cherokee's main drag also featured a Te-pee Motel, but in this case the conical shape was confined to the sign out front, not the building.

Mac's Indian Village — at the Entrance to the Cherokee Indian Reservation and the

Photo by Cline Studios   Great Smoky Mt's Nat'l Park. On Highway N. C. 107. E. Cherokee, N. C.   69376

CLOCKWISE FROM LEFT:

Mac's Indian Village opened in Cherokee in 1934, with conical tepee shapes attached to the front of each cabin. (Warren Reed Collection)

By the autumn of 2005, Mac's Indian Village sat in a deteriorated condition and appeared to be awaiting the wrecking ball. (Warren Reed Collection)

Cherokee's Chief Motel fit into the surrounding theme like a comfortable old pair of moccasins.

The boom that hit Cherokee with the arrival of the casino industry spelled doom for most of the other small motels that employed Indian themes. Near the Harrah's Casino was the quaint Chief Motel, with its neon sign featuring the same type of chiefs who had photos taken with tourists. Early photos show the sign with only the head and chest of said tribal official; later photos show an arm with pointing hand added, perhaps to guide drivers into the parking lot. Across the street, the Princess Motel had the neon chief's daughter on its sign. Like Mac's Indian Village, in the fall of 2005 both the Chief and the Princess sat abandoned, awaiting the bulldozers and new, more modern uses for their property.

The most famous of the surviving Cherokee motels did not use Indian symbols, although that probably has nothing to do with its longevity. The Pink Motel has attained a sort of cult status among roadside history buffs because of its immaculately maintained neon sign spectacular. The wand-wielding pixie on the sign could well have been mistaken for the Disney version of Peter Pan's companion Tinker Bell (which would date it to sometime after 1953, when that animated feature was released). However, since we know the owners of the Pink Motel would never want to run afoul of the dreaded Disney legal department, let's do the beneficent thing and say that this sprite's name was Pinker Bell. Happy now, Captain Hook?

Besides the sprightly signage, the Pink Motel carried out its name in every other conceivable way, with the rosy color splashed all over the place. Helping to provide an air of serenity, the back porch of each room overlooked a small stream. As of 2006, the Pink Motel remained in the pink, so long may the ponytailed pixie's wand wave.

The area surrounding Lookout Mountain and its varied attractions developed its own cast of characters in the motel scenario. Most of the ones that clustered around the base of the mountain did not go after any sort of theme in particular, unless one counts their

Cherokee's Pink Motel has become a roadside legend because of this immaculately maintained neon beauty of a sign.

During the 1960s, the Pink Motel and its neighbor, Newfound Lodge—owned by the same people—promoted the nearby *Unto These Hills* drama on their placemats.

similar architectural styles. Small but typical was the Lynmac Motel, whose name made little sense unless one learned from the postcards that the owner's name was Aline McNamara. The Lynmac had the good fortune to be located at the intersection where four major tourist routes into Chattanooga—U.S. 11, U.S. 41, U.S. 64, and U.S. 72—converged to become a single highway. With its buildings surfaced in rockwork and a manicured lawn complete with white picket fence, the Lynmac presented a most inviting air. Progress, however, waits for no invitation, and at last report only four abandoned rooms remained standing as the construction of a Wal-Mart Superstore took place around them.

Atop Lookout Mountain itself, some motels tried hard to fit into the prevailing attractions. The Fairyland Court was only seven blocks from the entrance to Rock City and played up that point with its logo of a chubby elf who resembled Happy of the Seven Dwarfs. The Fairyland Court advertised that it was approved by Duncan Hines—which was fine and dandy, but more importantly, what did Mother Goose have to say about it? Meanwhile, the Lookout Mountain Tourist Lodge used a neon depiction of an Indian seated on his horse, perched on a Lookout overlook and looking out.

In the days before freeways and interstate highways, since getting there was half the fun—or half the aggravation, depending on your attitude—even motels located on the heavily traveled tourist routes got creative. Such efforts obviously sought to get more people to stop and stay and spend a while but also helped travelers who had been on the road for extended periods feel that they were getting somewhere. For instance, the Log Cabin Court in Pulaski, Tennessee, followed the example set in Gatlinburg and elsewhere of having tourist cabins built from logs—with a name like Log Cabin Court, you were expecting vinyl siding? Even though Pulaski was almost halfway across Tennessee from the Great Smokies, drivers heading in that direction could get a preview of what was to come.

The postcards sent home by friends lucky enough to be on the road also provide an all-too-brief peek into those less hurried days. A postcard from the Milestone Court in Asheville—consisting of stone cabins instead of the log type—was mailed on June 13, 1950, with the comments, "Never have I seen anything any more beautiful than the mountains around Asheville. If the Smoky Mountains are any prettier, I can't describe it. Don't know what we are going to do today. Don't know our route yet. But will be in the Smoky Mountains reservation sometime tomorrow. Love, Nell."

Chain motels invaded all of the mountain resorts beginning in the early 1960s, but unlike some other areas, they never outnumbered the smaller, homier kind. Holiday Inn and its colorful signage could be found in Gatlinburg and the highways that led there. A wonderful photo of the lobby of the Holiday Inn in Cleveland, Tennessee, is almost overwhelming in its detail, from the statue of fictional innkeeper John Holiday holding a lighted lantern to the brochure rack holding colorful advertisements for Rock City, Ruby Falls, the Confederama, and other area sights. Other chains such as Howard Johnson's—which had long been a presence in restaurant circles in the area—and Best Western later joined the fun.

And, as with the attractions we visited in earlier chapters, mixed in among all of these were a few motels that just somehow did not seem to fit their surroundings. Chief among these was the Smoky Mt. Plaza in Gatlinburg. What was wrong with that, you say? Wasn't that the perfect name for a motel in its location? Yes, the name was fine—but the fact that the motel was painted aqua with pink trim made it more suited for the beach. The Rainbow Motel, also in Gatlinburg, sounded like something that should have been found near Florida's Rainbow Springs. And somehow, it is difficult to imagine getting a worry-free rest at a place called the Hemlock Motel. Perhaps that was where people went for the sleep that never ends. (Okay, the

motel was named after the species of pine tree common in the area, not the notorious poisonous plant, but it made a pretty good gag, anyway.)

Turning serious, that sort of fear eventually came true, even if not at the Hemlock. Gatlinburg motels made headlines of the type no one wanted in September 1986, when the Rocky Top Village Inn became the scene of a hideous murder that ultimately seemed to involve most of the surrounding tourism empire. Desk clerk Missy Hill and night watchman Troy Valentine were found shot and stabbed to death near the motel office. Suspicions immediately centered on a Harley-Davidson bikers' rally taking place in Cherokee that week that had spilled over the mountains into Gatlinburg. Someone found an unsigned confession note in a phone booth at Maggie Valley, but the case at first seemed to be going nowhere for Gatlinburg police department detective Bud Parton—and no one has to point out the name of his most famous relative and her own theme park. When

ABOVE: Yes, this was how Pigeon Forge appeared at one time. Across the street from the Bilmar Motor Inn can be glimpsed the entrance to Goldrush Junction and the adjoining Cross Ties Restaurant.

LEFT: "Chief" Henry Lambert's stoic profile was used to advertise the Boundary Tree Lodge in Cherokee in 1966.

Owned & Operated By The
EASTERN BAND
of CHEROKEE
INDIANS

BOUNDARY TREE
LODGE
DINING ROOM

BOUNDARY TREE LODGE - MOTEL
Cherokee, N. C., on U. S. 441 at Southern Entrance to Great Smoky Mountains National Park
62 deluxe units, each with air conditioning, TV, wall to wall carpeting and individually controlled heat. Pool. One half mile from Drama, "Unto These Hills". Owned and operated by the Eastern Band of Cherokee Indians. P. O. Box 464, Phone
P. O. Box 464   Phone 497-2155

With the right lighting and camera angles, colorful neon can present a slightly eerie or foreboding appearance.

justice finally caught up with the perpetrators, one commentator remarked that they looked like exhibits from the Ripley's Believe It or Not! Museum. The quartet of drifters from Atlanta consisted of an ex-con and hustler with more than one hundred tattoos covering his body, a hooker, and a transvestite and his male lover. All were eventually convicted and put away, but the incident shook the area's motel industry to its very foundations. The only fortunate thing, if there could be one, is that it garnered so much attention precisely because such crimes were so rare in the area.

The lurid 1986 Rocky Top murders caused many business owners to band together to combat such threats, but on the attractions side—where crime was less of a major concern—some cooperation had been going on for nearly thirty years.

Tourist attractions had previously been subject to a number of petty rivalries, both real and imagined. In the late 1950s, with the total number of tourists on the roads greater than ever before (plus the threat that the newfangled interstate highways would take business away from the old tourist routes), it seemed to be time for the attractions to work together rather than against each other. This feeling led to the formation of the Southern Highlands Attractions association (SHA).

Although not specifically stated, the SHA was likely modeled on the Florida Attractions Association, begun in 1949. Both groups had similar ways of doing things, despite the vast differences in marketing Florida and marketing the mountain attractions. Each SHA member paid an annual fee, and these funds were used to produce advertising materials that would promote all of the member attractions.

SHA was officially established when its first meeting was held at the Fairyland Club on Lookout Mountain on February 22, 1957. Carl Gibson of Ruby Falls was elected to serve as the first president,

This group portrait of Southern Highlands Attractions representatives captures many of the individuals responsible for the fun sites visited in this book. *Front row*: John Parris (*Unto These Hills*); Ed Chapin (Rock City); Spencer Robbins (Tweetsie Railroad and Blowing Rock); Bob Harsberger (Luray Caverns); Dyer Butterfield (Lookout Mountain Incline); Lou Harshaw (Asheville Chamber of Commerce); Hugh Morton (Grandfather Mountain). *Back row:* Tom Erwin and Carl Gibson (Ruby Falls); Dick Borden (Rock City); R. L. Maples (*Chucky Jack*); Norman Greig (Chimney Rock); O. A. Fetch and Paul Spirko (Fontana Village); Bart Leiper (Gatlinburg Sky Lift); Leo Derrick (*Horn in the West*). (Hugh Morton Collection)

207

This early 1980s Southern Highlands Attractions artwork deftly blends the trademark images of most of its member attractions into a single painting. Now that you have gotten this far, you should be able to identify most of them.

SOUTHERN HIGHLANDS

ATTRACTIONS

Scenic and Historic Landmarks

Southern Highlands Attractions

18 SIGHTS TO SEE.....

and at that first meeting the charter members were accepted: Rock City, Ruby Falls, and the Lookout Mountain Incline; Virginia's Luray Caverns and Natural Bridge; the outdoor dramas *Unto These Hills*, *Horn in the West*, and *Chucky Jack*; the Gatlinburg Sky Lift; and North Carolina's Oconaluftee Indian Village, Fontana Dam, Thomas Wolfe Memorial, Chimney Rock Park, Grandfather Mountain, Blowing Rock, and Tweetsie Railroad. While other attractions would be added over the years and some of the originals would drop out, most of these charter members still constitute the SHA's core today.

The attractions found that SHA provided many benefits not otherwise available. Each attraction displayed the brochures of all the others as well as a framed map showing their locations. In a move that would have been almost unheard of in the old days, attractions often recommended each other to their patrons—Ruby Falls would suggest that their visitors "See Rock City" after finishing their tour of the caverns, and vice versa. While some rivalries continued in private, at least publicly the various tourist attractions gave the image of all playing on the same team.

Because the Great Smoky Mountains National Park is the most visited in the National Park system, this sign is said to have been photographed more than any other sight in the system.

Although some residents complain about Gatlinburg's transformation from a rural mountain village into what some have called the Las Vegas of the South, at the end of the day the tourists drive the local economy.

The SHA and its activities remain strong among today's attractions, but the region recently has relied more and more on slick media advertising. Especially in the spring and fall, television viewers are inundated with commercials promoting the Great Smoky Mountains National Park and the area in general. Some of these ads rely on tourism nostalgia to make their point, such as one that depicted several generations of tourists posing in front of the seemingly unchanging park entrance sign from the black and white 1950s to the present day. Others used the unmistakable figure of Dolly Parton to lure in the travelers, while another campaign for area motels was built around an actor in a comical black bear costume with an incongruously "normal" voice provided by actor Kyle Holman ("If you're going to the mountains, it only makes sense to stay in the mountains").

But at the end of the day, the Land of the Smokies really does not seem to require any advertising at all. After all, it has been building a reputation and goodwill for at least a century—even longer in some spots. While some natives continue to grouse about the traffic congestion and the transformation of former hamlets such as Gatlinburg into carnivals of the bizarre, the tourists seem to be getting exactly what they want. And, in the opinion of those who make their living off of those visitors' spending habits, it is not only what they want but exactly what they deserve.

YA'LL COME BACK NOW, Y'HEAR?

Bibliography

Published Sources

Auchmutey, Jim. "See Rock City: The Story behind the Slogan." *Atlanta Journal-Constitution*, May 10, 1992.

Baeder, John. *Gas, Food, and Lodging*. New York: Abbeville, 1982.

Bennett, Rod. "Stranger Than You Think: Ripley's Believe It or Not!" *Wonder Magazine*, Summer 1996.

Blast from the Past: The History of Tweetsie Railroad. Blowing Rock, N.C.: Tweetsie Railroad, n.d.

Brinkley, Ed. *The History of Ruby Falls*. Chattanooga: Brinkley, 1980.

Capps, Anita Armstrong. *See Rock City Barns: A Tennessee Tradition*. Chattanooga: See Rock City, 1996.

"Chamber of Commerce Tourist Boosters Open War on Guides." *Chattanooga Free Press*, January 28, 1938.

"Charge of Racketeering Methods by Lookout Guides Brings Denial." *Chattanooga Times*, January 20, 1938.

"Crafts Helped Mold Sevier County." *Mountain Visitor*, June 15, 1981.

"Debbie Reynolds Brings Hollywood to Tennessee." Associated Press, March 8, 2004.

Edge, Lynn. "Classy Mandrell to End Her Run." *Birmingham News*, July 3, 2005.

"Found: The Lost Sea." *Southern Living*, November 1968.

Garber, Anna. "Aquarium Has Dramatic Impact on Revenue." *Mountain Press*, December 1, 2001.

Hamilton, Virginia van der Veer. "Before the Freeway, There Was U.S. 11." *New York Times*, November 23, 1986.

Harkins, Anthony. *Hillbilly: A Cultural History of an American Icon*. New York: Oxford University Press, 2004.

Harmetz, Aljean. *The Making of the Wizard of Oz*. New York: Knopf, 1977.

"He Needed a Hobby, So He Builds Dinosaurs." Associated Press, March 23, 1972.

Hollis, Tim. *Dixie before Disney: 100 Years of Roadside Fun*. Jackson: University Press of Mississippi, 1999

———. *Florida's Miracle Strip: From Redneck Riviera to Emerald Coast*. Jackson: University Press of Mississippi, 2004.

———. *Glass Bottom Boats and Mermaid Tails: Florida's Tourist Springs*. Mechanicsburg, Pa.: Stackpole, 2006.

———. *Hi There, Boys and Girls! America's Local Children's TV Programs*. Jackson: University Press of Mississippi, 2001.

———. *Six Flags Over Georgia*. Mount Pleasant, S.C.: Arcadia, 2006.

Hollis, Tim, and Greg Ehrbar. *Mouse Tracks: The Story of Walt Disney Records*. Jackson: University Press of Mississippi, 2006.

"James Sidwell, Dinosaur Man." *Mountain Visitor*, June 15, 1981.

Jenkins, David B. *Rock City Barns: A Passing Era*. Chattanooga: Free Spirit, 1996.

Jennings, Jan, ed. *Roadside America: The Automobile in Design and Culture*. Ames: Iowa State University Press, 1990.

Kenyon, Nellie. "Carters Develop Beautiful Park in Rock City on Lookout Mtn." *Chattanooga News*, May 13, 1932.

Lammon, Pat. "Sevier Businessmen Get Set for Tourists." *Sevier County News-Record*, May 9, 1978.

Leiper, Bart. *The Story of Gatlinburg's Christus Gardens*. Gatlinburg: Christus Biblical Gardens, 1967.

Liebs, Chester. *Main Street to Miracle Mile: American Roadside Architecture*. Baltimore: Johns Hopkins University Press, 1995.

Long, Travis. "Chiefly for the Tourists." *Charlotte News-Observer*, September 4, 2005.

Malone, Bill C., and Judith McCulloh. *Stars of Country Music: Uncle Dave Macon to Johnny Rodriguez*. Urbana: University of Illinois Press, 1975.

Margolies, John. *Fun along the Road: American Tourist Attractions*. Boston: Little, Brown, 1998.

———. *Miniature Golf*. New York: Abbeville, 1987.

Margolies, John, and Emily Gwathmey. *Signs of Our Time*. New York: Abbeville, 1993.

Martin, Christopher. *Your National Parks: Great Smoky Mountains*. New York: Putnam's, 1965.

McDowell, Edwin. "Nature Is Second Fiddle to Dolly's Theme Park." *New York Times*, August 14, 1997.

Medlin, Patricia Kirby. *Fred Kirby: A Tribute*. Maggie Valley, N.C.: Sidekick, 1998.

Morton, Hugh. *Hugh Morton's North Carolina*. Chapel Hill: University of North Carolina Press, 2003.

———. *Mildred the Bear*. Linville, N.C.: Morton, 1999.

"Mysterious Mansion Comes to Gatlinburg." *Mountain Visitor*, June 15, 1981.

"New 1981 Tommy Bartlett's Water Circus." *Mountain Visitor*, June 15, 1981.

"New Addition in Golf Available in Pigeon Forge." *Mountain Visitor*, June 15, 1981.

Oakley, Wiley. *Roamin' with the Roamin' Man of the Smoky Mountains*. Gatlinburg: Little Pigeon, 1940.

"Outdoor Dramas Re-Create History." *Southern Living*, July 1966.

Pirtle, Caleb, III. "We're Off to See the Wizard." *Southern Living*, June 1971.

Preston, Howard Lawrence. *Dirt Roads to Dixie*. Knoxville: University of Tennessee Press, 1991.

Seig, Tom. "High Adventure in the Land of Oz." *Holiday Inn Magazine*, July 1970.

"Silver Dollar City: A 'Must See' Attraction." *Mountain Visitor*, July 17, 1978.

Starnes, Richard D. *Creating the Land of the Sky: Tourism and Society in Western North Carolina.* Tuscaloosa: University of Alabama Press, 2005.

Stern, Jane, and Michael Stern. *The Encyclopedia of Bad Taste.* New York: HarperCollins, 1990.

Stone, Dean. "Kermit Caughron: Won't Celebrate." *Knoxville Daily Times,* February 24, 1984.

Stone, Mary O. "The New Wonderland Hotel Continues Traditions." *Experienced Living,* February 15, 1993.

"Tourist Spots Where It Is—and Isn't—Happening." *Wall Street Journal,* April 17, 1996.

Trout, Ed. *Gatlinburg: Cinderella City.* Pigeon Forge: Griffin, 1984.

Vernon, Kerry. "A Visit with the Last of the Gatlins." *Mountain Visitor,* June 15, 1981.

Waggoner, Susan. *It's a Wonderful Christmas: The Best of the Holidays, 1940–1965.* New York: Stewart, Tabori, and Chang, 2004.

"What's New at Magic World?" *Mountain Visitor,* July 17, 1978.

Williamson, J. W. *Hillbillyland: What the Movies Did to the Mountains and What the Mountains Did to the Movies.* Chapel Hill: University of North Carolina Press, 1995.

Wilson, John. *Lookout: The Story of an Amazing Mountain.* Chattanooga: Wilson, 1977.

Zimmerman, Elena Irish. *Sevierville, Gatlinburg, and Maryville.* Mount Pleasant, S.C.: Arcadia, 1996.

Unpublished Sources

Hollis, Tim. "See Rock City: The Story of Rock City Gardens Atop Lookout Mountain." 1992. In possession of author.

Jones, James B. "The Development of Motor Tourism in Tennessee's Southeastern Corridor, 1910–1945." Tennessee Historical Commission, 1991. In possession of the author.

Weyman, Grant. "The Life of Garnet Carter." 1975. In Rock City Collection.

Film and Video Sources

City Confidential: Gatlinburg, Tennessee. A&E Network, 2001.

Greetings from Forgotten Florida. New River Media, 2000.

Southern Highlands: America's Pictureland. Eastman Kodak Company and
Southern Highlands Attractions, 1979.

Interviews and Correspondence

Gene Aiken, Shelby Boyd, Phil Campbell, Dave Carr, Jim Cary, Elsie Cole,
Mabel Ellis, Kassie Hassler, Cindy Keller, Gary Kimble, Veta King, Henry
Lambert, Ronald Ligon, Ted Miller, Hugh Morton, Pete Owens, Mark
Pedro, Fred Pfohl, Harris Prevost, Chris Robbins, Harry Robbins, Spen-
cer Robbins, Jim Sidwell Jr., Andy Smalls, Richard Starnes, Richard
Swan, Earlene Teaster, Hugh Thomas, Charles Tombras, Joe Waggoner,
Charles Watkins, Linda Whittington, Robert Young

Index